A
TRAVELLER'S
WINE GUIDE
TO

France

A TRAVELLER'S WINE GUIDE TO

France

Christopher Fielden

Additional material by Jim Budd

Foreword by Kerry Brady Stewart

Photographs by Michel Brioul
and Janet Price

INTERLINK BOOKS
An imprint of Interlink Publishing Group, Inc.
New York

This revised and updated edition first published 2000 by **Interlink Books**, an imprint of Interlink Publishing Group, Inc., 99 Seventh Avenue, Brooklyn, New York 11215.

Edited by Keith Bambury, Philip Clark and Tony Raven

Photographs by Michel Brioul and Janet Price (except where otherwise credited)

Maps by AND Map Graphics Ltd., Carte Blanche Ltd., Andrew Green and Simon Green

Copyright © Philip Clark Ltd., 1989, 1997, 2000

Library of Congress Cataloging-in-Publication Data
Fielden, Christopher.
  A traveller's wine guide to France/ Christopher Fielden:
  photographs by Michel Brioul and Janet Price.
    p.   cm. – (Traveller's wine guides)
  Includes bibliographical references and index.
    ISBN 1-56656-352-6 (pbk, : alk paper)
  1. Wine and wine making – France – Guidebooks. 2. France – Guidebooks.
  I. Title. 2. Series.
  TP553.F5 1997
  641.2'2'0944 –dc20
                              98-45974
                                   CIP

The *Traveller's Wine Guides* were conceived and produced by Philip Clark Ltd., 53 Calton Avenue, London SE21 7DF, U.K.

Printed in Singapore for Imago

ACKNOWLEDGEMENTS

The author and publisher would particularly like to thank the following for their help in the preparation of this book:

For reading the text and contributing valuable suggestions: Philippe Boucheron, Jean Bourgeois, Françoise le Labourier and Kerry Brady Stewart.

Keith Bambury for his technical assistance, Tony Raven for his help in editing the text and preparing the index, and Helen White for word-processing the original manuscript.

Among the organizations that have supplied illustrations and provided information are: The French Government Tourist Office, French Railways Ltd., Moët & Chandon (London) Ltd., Peretti Communications Ltd., and Sopexa Ltd.

COVER

Designed by Studio Two

Main illustration: Autumnal colours among Pinot Noir vines near Ville-Dommange on the Montagne de Reims, Champagne. (Photograph: Mick Rock/Cephas Picture Library)

Foreground photography by Darius

TITLE ILLUSTRATION

Dusk over the vineyards of Châteauneuf-du-Pape, with the river Rhône in the distance. (Photograph: Mick Rock/Cephas Picture Library)

ARTWORK

Clive Spong/Linden Artists Ltd.: 14

PHOTO CREDITS

Michel Brioul 6/7, 15, 18, 19, 20, 21, 22/23, 23, 26, 28, 29, 30, 31, 32, 33, 41, 50/51, 53, 54, 55, 57, 58(2), 61, 62, 64, 65, 66, 68, 70, 71, 72, 74, 78(2), 79, 83, 84, 87, 90, 91, 92, 94/95, 97, 99, 100, 101, 102, 103, 104, 105, 107, 108, 109, 111, 114, 115, 116, 117, 118, 119, 120, 124/125 (below), 126

Janet Price 12/13, 25, 34, 38, 38/39, 42, 44, 45, 47, 48, 49, 52, 69, 73, 85

Comité Interprofessionel des Vins d'Origine du Pays Nantais 86

Patrick Eagar 36, 40, 46, 60, 81

Elf Oil (UK Ltd.) 12

French Government Tourist Office 128

Moët & Chandon (London) Ltd. 16 (above)

Mick Rock/Cephas Picture Library 13

Sopexa Ltd. 133

Francesco Venturi 16 (below)

Alan Williams 75, 97

Zefa Picture Library 111, 122, 124/125 (above)

Contents

How to Use this Book

This book is designed for the visitor to France who wants to see how wine is made, to taste it and, possibly, to buy it. While wine can be bought in shops, and tasted in restaurants, in France it is the cellars that count.

In some towns – Beaune is a notable example – there are a number of shops specializing in the sale of the local wines. For the most part, however, French people buy their wine in supermarkets, or direct from the grower. Their contact with a grower may be through a representative who will come to the door with samples. It may be by an annual visit to the vineyard to talk and to taste. It may be by buying at one of the many regional fairs, where there will be wine-stands.

Visiting vineyards

This book is mainly about vineyard visiting, though a number of local wine fairs are listed, with approximate dates. These are wonderful events for tasting and comparing, though the chances of purchasing more than the odd bottle or two on the spot are small, as most of the orders taken are for subsequent delivery. I would not recommend this method of buying wine, however. Direct importation is best left to the professionals.

As you travel through France, you can dip into the book to find basic information about the local wines, the names and addresses of some of the local growers and merchants and places of interest, such as wine museums.

For most areas, too, there is the address of the office of the body looking after the promotion of the local wines. Here they will probably have available complete lists of local growers and detailed wine maps of the region.

Tourist offices

I can also recommend a visit to the local tourist office. (Details of many of these in the wine regions appear on page 140). They are invariably helpful and they can usually come up with some individual or topical advice.

In addition, if you wish to know about the basic driving regulations in France, how many gallons a grower produces when he talks in liters or the best way of buying wine to bring home, it is all here in this book.

Wine touring

This book is structured around the French motorway system (which is why part of the Loire valley appears in the chapter on Burgundy), but when you have arrived at your destination, please do not drink and drive.

While this book is designed to be as self-contained as possible, it cannot take the place of a road atlas. For detailed maps showing short cuts or scenic routes, I would suggest that the wine-loving motorist should also buy the *Michelin Motoring Atlas of France*.

One of the pleasures of wine touring is the limitless interest of the subject. Each year the wine is different, each season the scenery changes. Around every corner there is a new grower or merchant waiting to be visited. This book will give you an introduction to just a few of them. It is a beginning, but by no means the whole. I hope that for the newcomer to vineyard visiting it will open the first doors and, for the hardened regular, it will provide some new addresses.

There can be few more satisfying ways of passing time in France than talking to a grower about his or her wine, with a glass of it in your hand. I hope that this book will help you to achieve this satisfaction.

INFORMATION PANEL SYMBOLS

TF	Tastings are free
TP	Tastings must be paid for
WS	Wine for sale
D	Danish spoken
E	English spoken
G	German spoken
I	Italian spoken
N	Dutch spoken
S	Spanish spoken
☏	Telephoning in advance advisable
☎	Appointment must be made in advance by telephone or fax

NOTE: Where practicable, it is a good idea to contact the grower in advance of a visit, not only out of politeness, but also to check that nothing has changed since the information in this book was compiled. (See the notes on how to use a French telephone, and the model letter/fax in French, on page 141.)

Foreword

by Kerry Brady Stewart

What a wonderful way to become acquainted with the landscape, people and traditions of a country – discovering wines at their source. Where there's good wine, good food is rarely absent. France is famous for both.

The sheer number of interesting people and places to visit can seem overwhelming. Especially for those with only a week or two for a trip, Christopher Fielden's suggestions will be invaluable when planning an itinerary, both before leaving home and en route, while travelling through France's wine country.

Drawing on his own experience in the wine trade and many years of visits to the vineyards of France, Fielden is well-suited to provide excellent advice on how and where to visit vineyards and cellars. He shares a wealth of information about the local wines – in layman's terms – and points out historical and cultural details that add to the pleasure of any trip.

On the basis of my own visits to France, I can only echo Christopher Fielden's enthusiasm about the hospitality of wine growers and the pleasure of what he aptly calls vineyard visiting: a voyage of discovery.

The walled cité (Old Town) of Carcassonne, in south-eastern France, viewed across a green sea of vines. The medieval ramparts were painstakingly restored in the 1840s by Viollet-le-Duc.

Introduction

France is no longer regularly the world's largest producer of wine, nor does it have the largest area under vines. Those distinctions belong to Italy and Spain respectively. Nevertheless, it is to France that the consumer tends to look for quality. Although wine is now being made throughout the world, French wines still provide the benchmark against which many producers in other countries assess their output.

This is no coincidence, for it is in France that the broadest variety of wines is made. You can find every style of wine there if you are prepared to look for it: not just the classic wines of Bordeaux and Burgundy, but also such rarities as Château Chalon from the Jura, which rivals the finest fino sherry.

There is always something new to see and taste, and there can be no more hospitable vocation than that of wine producer. Whether you speak French or not, if you are interested in the end product, the producer will make you welcome.

This book should be particularly helpful to motorists who are interested in visiting some of the vineyards of France while they are driving through, as it is based on the motorway system, which radiates out from Paris in all directions. For readers approaching France from the U.K., the A26 now provides a more rapid route to the South and East.

Many of the most important wine regions lie close to the motorways – who can forget the first sight of the vineyards of Burgundy when the A6 swoops down on the town of Beaune? With the help of this book, you can choose where to leave the main roads to break off and spend as little or as much time as you like, with glass in hand talking to the grower about his wines.

I do not know how many hundreds of thousands of wine-makers there are in France. This book can give but a small selection. The choice has been mine – but each has said that he or she will make visitors welcome.

Some are no more than individual growers who might perhaps work the soil and make the wine with no more help than that of their immediate family. Others are multinational companies whose brands are household names around the world and whose cellars welcome hundreds of thousands of visitors each year.

I must admit that I have tried to avoid the "tourist traps", of which there are some in every vineyard region. Even in areas where the big brands dominate, like Champagne and Cognac, I have included some smaller family businesses.

Vineyard-visiting is a voyage of discovery. In researching this book, I have been to places that I have never been to before and I have made a host of new friends. I hope that readers, too, will discover much. There can be no country that has as broad a range of wines as France and it is often away from the well-beaten paths that the most pleasure is to be obtained.

The System of Classification

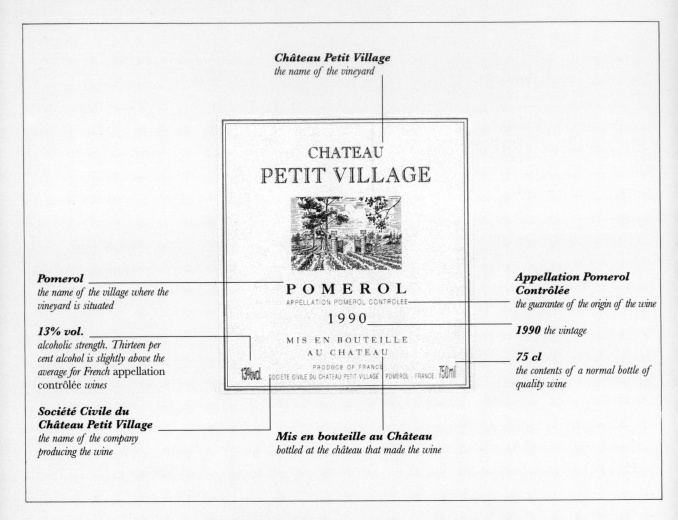

Château Petit Village
the name of the vineyard

CHATEAU
PETIT VILLAGE

POMEROL
APPELLATION POMEROL CONTROLEE
1990
MIS EN BOUTEILLE
AU CHATEAU
PRODUCE OF FRANCE
13%vol. SOCIETE CIVILE DU CHATEAU PETIT VILLAGE · POMEROL · FRANCE 750ml

Pomerol
the name of the village where the vineyard is situated

13% vol.
alcoholic strength. Thirteen per cent alcohol is slightly above the average for French appellation contrôlée wines

Société Civile du Château Petit Village
the name of the company producing the wine

Appellation Pomerol Contrôlée
the guarantee of the origin of the wine

1990 *the vintage*

75 cl
the contents of a normal bottle of quality wine

Mis en bouteille au Château
bottled at the château that made the wine

All the wines of France are classified according to a rigid hierarchy, depending on the potential quality of the wine. At the bottom comes the simple *vin de table*. This may come from anywhere in France, and is generally blended from a variety of sources, mainly from within France itself, though other wines made in the European Union can be blended in if the fact is mentioned on the label.

This is the wine for everyday drinking, sold in plastic bottles or the ubiquitous, returnable, six-star liter bottles. It will have no vintage, and the label will generally give no more than a brand name and the alcoholic degree of the wine.

Vins de Pays
One step up the ladder come the *vins de pays*. For these wines there are strict controls on the quantity that may be produced per hectare, the grapes that are used and their source. The region of production may be quite small, for example, the Vin de Pays des Coteaux de Peyriac; from one *département*, like a Vin de Pays de l'Aude; or from a much wider area like a Vin de Pays du Pays d'Oc.

Occasionally there are surprises to be found when a grower will experiment with a classic grape variety where it has not previously been grown. Particular examples are the Cabernet Sauvignon, the Chardonnay and the Syrah. Such wines can now be found in the Rhône valley, Provence and Languedoc-Roussillon.

Superior quality wines

Higher up the scale come VDQS wines. The letters stand for *Vin Délimité de Qualité Supérieure* (superior quality wine). These are sometimes traditional regional wines, like the acid rosé wines of Lorraine called Côtes de Toul, and sometimes wines that are progressing up the ranks. Here the controls on production are more strict – and the prices higher.

At the top of the ladder come the *appellation contrôlée* wines. I say at the top of the ladder, but there one finds a broad platform, which will include wines that have recently been promoted from VDQS status, like Coteaux de Giennois, and some of the greatest and most expensive wines in the world, like Romanée-Conti from Burgundy.

The label

Whatever the French wine, its classification will appear on the label. Thus you can tell easily where it stands in the classification scale. A word of warning, however: the rating is not necessarily related to quality, but more to the controls that have been made on the production. It is possible to find excellent, and expensive, *vins de table*. Perhaps the vineyard is the wrong place, perhaps the vines are too young or the grape variety is not accepted in the region.

Surely, here lies one of the real attractions of visiting the growers – the opportunity of discovering a wine that belies its status. Good hunting!

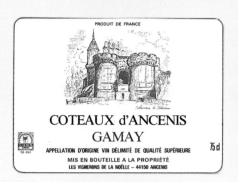

PRODUIT DE FRANCE

COTEAUX d'ANCENIS
GAMAY
APPELLATION D'ORIGINE VIN DÉLIMITÉ DE QUALITÉ SUPÉRIEURE   75 cl
MIS EN BOUTEILLE A LA PROPRIÉTÉ
LES VIGNERONS DE LA NOËLLE – 44150 ANCENIS

Domaine des Embasties

SAUVIGNON

VIN DE PAYS D'OC

1994

MIS EN BOUTEILLE
PAR CELLIERS JEAN D'ALIBERT
A F. 11 160 . PEYRIAC
75 cl   PRODUIT DE FRANCE   12% vol.

PRODUCE OF FRANCE

Cuvée d'Adrien

MEDIUM

VIN DE TABLE
FRANÇAIS

MIS EN BOUTEILLE
PAR CHANTOVENT SA À
78270 BONNIÈRES FRANCE
SELECTED BY
100 cl   LAY & WHEELER   11+1.5% vol
COLCHESTER ENGLAND

Vin Délimité de Qualité Supérieure (VDQS)

The special seal for this category of wine appears in the bottom left-hand corner of the label. Also shown is the grape variety from which it is made – the Gamay. The Coteaux d'Ancenis are on the north bank of the river Loire, just to the east of Nantes.

Vin de Pays

This is still a table wine, but it comes from a specific region, the Pays d'Oc, or Languedoc. The label also gives the vintage.

Vin de Table

The source of the wine is shown simply as France. The strength of the wine is shown in the bottom right-hand corner. As this is a sweet wine, the label gives not only the alcoholic degree, but also the potential strength that would be added if the residual sugar were fermented out. There can be no mention of vintage, grape variety or the exact origin of table wine.

Travelling in France

A French motorway service station. Automat *is a cafeteria;* Libre service *means self-service; and* Poids Lourds *(literally "heavy weights") are heavy goods vehicles.*

Motorways

For the most part, motoring in France is not difficult. There is a broad motorway system that can enable considerable distances to be covered in a short time. On the motorways, there are frequent rest areas and numerous restaurants where one can eat and drink reasonably. The sign *Aire* means an open-air stopping place or picnic site.

The cost of motorway tolls can mount up, however, and, if speed is not important, there are generally main roads that run in parallel. These can, however, be crowded with heavy vehicles also intent on avoiding the tolls.

In any case, all roads are to be avoided at the beginning and end of holiday periods, even holiday weekends, as traffic jams appear to be endemic. Alternative long-distance routes are marked with green signs.

Gasoline

Gasoline is expensive in France. At the pumps you will find Super 98 *sans plomb* (unleaded), 95 octane unleaded, Super (with lead) and Diesel, which is significantly cheaper than Super.

Generally, money can be saved by filling up at hypermarkets. All of them have gas pumps, and credit cards are almost universally accepted. Eurocheques are still accepted in France, but it is much easier to pay by credit card at service stations.

Car rental

For those considering renting a car, a word of warning: rental cars are liable to a luxury rate of value added tax and can become very expensive. It might well be worthwhile to rent one just across the border.

France by rail

Communications between Britain and France have been transformed by the Channel Tunnel, which provides a link between the two countries both for motorists and for rail travelers.

Paris is now three hours from London by rail. The other main Eurostar terminus in France is Lille, on the Franco-Belgian border. It is therefore possible to travel from Britain to France's wine-producing regions by Eurostar and TGV (High Speed Train) without passing through Paris.

Travelling at speeds of up to 300km/hr (186 mph) the TGV from Lille takes less than 3 hours to reach Dijon, the capital of Burgundy. The Loire valley is about 6 hours from London by rail and Bordeaux about 8 hours. Paris, is, however, still the hub of the French rail system, and most overnight trains leave from the French capital.

Hotels

Hotels are for the most part not expensive, though the bedrooms can be somewhat spartan. The Logis de France is a chain of independent family-run hotels. They are generally reasonably priced, clean and comfortable. There are also a number of chains of simple hotels, generally on the approaches to towns, which can be ideal for one-night stopovers with all rooms having private baths and television. They also have clean friendly restaurants, often with a buffet hors d'oeuvres, and simple grills as main courses. Three such chains with hotels all over France are Ibis, Campanile, and Climat de France. Finally, it is always wise to book your hotels in advance.

A minor road running through the Tronçais Forest in the Auvergne region of central France. This is the largest oak forest in Europe, and its timber is highly valued for making wine casks.

DRIVING IN FRANCE

Here are a few simple rules about driving in France. Driving is on the right and priority is on the right. In the open countryside, main roads always have priority, but beware of cars leaping out from the right in towns.

Until recently, cars coming into a roundabout always had priority, therefore often leading to a position of stalemate. This is now changing and there will be clear signs saying if you now do not have priority. The sign *Giratoire* before a roundabout indicates priority on the left.

Carry a full driving license, vehicle registration document and evidence of insurance cover. A Green Card is not always necessary, but for full cover you may need one. Consult your insurer.

Hazard warning lights or a red warning triangle and a spare set of bulbs must be carried. Seat belts must be worn in the front and rear seats of a car. Children under ten must not travel in the front, except in a two-seater.

An accident causing injury must be reported to the police and, after any other accident involving someone else, an accident report form should be filled in.

Fines for speeding and other traffic offences are heavy. Foreigners must pay a deposit of 900FF. Fines range from 900FF for exceeding the speed limit by 20-40km/hr (reduced to 600FF if paid on the spot) to 10,000FF for exceeding the speed limit by more than 50km/hr. These are levied in cash, although a cheque may be accepted with proof of identity, such as a passport.

In the case of drunk-driving offences, the car can also be impounded. The drink limit in France is now 0.5 grams of alcohol per liter of blood. Random breath tests occur, so do not consider driving after serious cellar visits!

Visiting a Winery

1. Hold the glass to the light to assess the wine's color.

2. Smell the wine.

3. Swirl the wine in the glass to liberate the flavor.

4. Sip the wine and move it around inside your mouth.

5. Spitting accurately is not easy. (Practise beforehand with a glass of water!)

Each visit suggested in this book will have its own particular character, and this may vary from day to day.

Some wineries particularly ask visitors to telephone in advance, in a few cases days in advance, and these are indicated by a telephone symbol. These are probably growers who are arranging to take time off from their work in the vineyards or the cellars to welcome you. They are not equipped to receive large parties. If for any reason you are unable to keep your appointment, or are going to be late, do please telephone to avoid people wasting their time.

Visiting hours

The blue information panels show the times when visitors are welcome. Check these carefully, as they often vary depending on the time of year.

It is important to realize that you need a reasonable amount of time for your visit, so don't arrive just before the last time shown. Either your visit will be cut short or you will be imposing on your host.

Don't visit at lunchtime!

Another matter to remember is that the French take their lunch seriously, so do not arrive too soon before – or after – the lunchtime closing.

At many of the smaller companies, there may well be no one who speaks English. Those places where English is spoken are indicated. Elsewhere, speak French if you can – even if it is rusty. The effort will certainly be appreciated and possibly even rewarded.

If, however, even this prospect alarms you, go armed with a good phrase-book, or better still, a French-speaking friend.

On the other hand, a number of firms are included that are used to receiving tourists and employ multi-lingual guides to look after the visitor. Here the welcome is likely to be less personal and to have a more commercial aspect.

French *vignerons* are among the most hospitable people in the world, but both their time and their stock are precious. Most growers are happy to offer you wine to taste free of charge, particularly if they think that you might buy some. Others charge for tasting and, again, this fact is mentioned in the reference panels.

Often, tasting charges are reimbursed with a purchase.

To spit or not to spit?

In order to keep a clear head when buying wine, it is best to spit out the tasting sample. A few glasses can soon persuade you that the wine is better than it is. Spitting the wine out is acceptable in all parts of France. If there is a spittoon (*un crachoir*) provided, make use of it; otherwise spit on the floor – if you are in a cellar, that is!

Generally, if more than one wine is offered for tasting, the quality will improve with each wine. Therefore most growers will be flattered if, with the last wine, you say that it is so good that you will not spit it out, but will drink it.

There are two further things to remember about tasting: first, a number of wines on an empty stomach can have a noticeable effect, so it is wise to take some ballast on board first. Secondly, drinking and driving is as serious an offense in France as elsewhere and your car can be impounded.

CALVADOS

Whilst there is nothing in the way of vineyards around the A13 motorway, which leads from the Channel ports of Caen, Le Havre and Dieppe to Paris, there are the apple orchards of Normandy, which produce the only non-grape spirit of France to have its own *appellation contrôlée*: Calvados.

Like the finest vineyard regions, the area is split into a number of smaller areas, each producing its own style of spirit. In all there are some eleven different regional appellations of Calvados, but the finest comes from the Pays d'Auge, which lies on both sides of the river Touques. This river flows into the English Channel at Deauville. The center of the region is Pont l'Evêque.

The Pays d'Auge Calvados is distilled from cider in exactly the same way as Cognac is made from wine. There is a double distillation in copper "pot" stills. The resultant spirit, which is approximately 70 per cent pure alcohol, has a distinct roughness, which is smoothed out by many years ageing in oak casks. The strength is then reduced before bottling and sale.

A number of the cellars and distilleries are open to the public and for those with rather more time on their hands, there is the Route du Cidre circuit. This is best joined by taking the D49 south from the Cabourg exit on the A13, or at Cambremer, which is off the D50, west of Lisieux. Farms on the circuit have a Cru de Cambremer sign.

CALVADOS
Domaine Coeur de Lion/ Christian Drouin S.A
Distillerie des Fiefs St. Anne, rte de Trouville, RN 177, 14130 Coudray-Rabut. Tel: 02 31 64 30 05. Fax: 02 31 64 35 62. Mon-Sat 0900-1200, 1400-1800. Calvados, cider, *pommeau* (aperitif). TF.WS.E.G.
S.A. Calvados Boulard
Moulin de la Foulonnerie, 14130 Coquainvilliers. Tel: 02 31 48 24 01. Fax: 02 31 62 21 22. Apr-Oct every day 0900-1230, 1400-1800. Nov-Mar Mon-Sat 1000-1200, 1400-1800. (Guided tours on request). TF.E.G.

MUSEUM
The Museum of Calvados and Ancient Crafts
Pont l'Evêque (on road to Deauville). Tel: 02 31 64 12 87. Fax: 02 31 65 44 75. Apr-Oct every day 1000-1200, 1430-1830. Nov-Mar shop only. TF (with entry charge). E.
FOR FURTHER INFORMATION
B.N.I.C.E. 31, rue St. Ouen, 14000 Caen. Tel: 02 31 75 30 90. Fax: 02 31 74 26 97.

To buy or not to buy?

Are you expected to buy some wine at the end of the visit? No way are you obliged to, but no grower can make a living by pouring limitless numbers of free glasses of wine. Certainly, there is less obligation if you have paid for your tasting.

If you do buy wine, you will pay French VAT (Value Added Tax) of 20.6 per cent. However, duties are much lower in France than in Britain, for example, and you should be able to make distinct savings.

Do you tip the person who shows you round? Certainly not if it is a family affair, but with a large company the palm of the guide might, at the end of the visit, be seen to hover. A small token would be appreciated.

Do remember that wine is heavy, and that a few cases add considerably to the weight of your car. As far as is practical, try to spread the load, and make sure that your tires have sufficient pressure.

Here's to many happy tastings.

Champagne

O f all the wine regions of France, Champagne is for many people the most readily accessible. Its centre, the ancient city of Reims, is an easy ninety minutes' drive along the motorway from Paris, and, for motorists from Britain, under three hours from the Channel Tunnel and ports.

For centuries, the still red wines of Champagne used to dispute with Burgundy the title of producing France's greatest wines and learned professors at the Sorbonne University in Paris would write papers on their rival merits. Whilst Champagne is now famous for its sparkling wines – indeed the word is accepted as a synonym for sparkling wine in many countries, including the United States – it was not until the beginning of the 18th century that the bubbling wine that we know today was first made in the region. Though Champagne is for the most part a white wine, it is made largely from a blend of red and white grapes. The red grapes come mainly from the valley of the Marne and the Montagne de Reims; the white from the Côte des Blancs.

The Champagne vineyards

On the map, the main vineyards of Champagne take the form of a double hook, with the shank lying along the valley of the river Marne. Here is the town of Epernay, where many of the great Champagne companies are based.

To the north, sweeping back in a loop, are the vineyards of the Montagne de Reims, with above them the town of Reims itself, its massive cathedral dominating the rolling countryside. Most of the other important names of Champagne have their cellars here.

The southern barb of the hook is known as the Côte des Blancs. There are also two other areas where Champagne is produced. To the north of Reims lies la Petite Montagne: many miles to the south-east are the remnants of what used to be the important vineyard area of the Aube.

Top left: This statue of Dom Perignon, the "inventor" of modern Champagne, stands outside the headquarters of Moët & Chandon in Epernay (see page 22). Below left: Visitors to the house of Pommery at Reims (see page 18) complete their tour of the cellars near this vast barrel, magnificently carved by Gallé.

There is now a renaissance of Champagne production here, but also a specialized rosé wine, Les Riceys, made from the Pinot Noir grape.

The skill in creating one of the great wines of Champagne lies in taking wines from a number of sources and styles, and putting them together to make a glorious whole. Now, whatever there is to celebrate, one calls for Champagne.

To get to Champagne
Reims is 142km (88 miles) E of Paris on the A4; 268 km (167 miles) S of Calais by the A26.

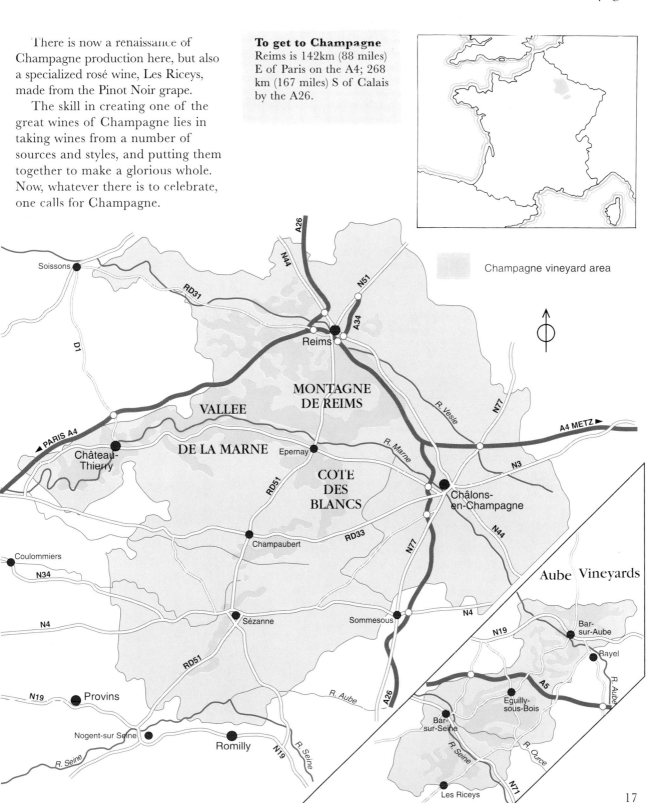

Champagne vineyard area

Aube Vineyards

Reims

REIMS

Champagne Piper Heidsieck 51, bvd Henri Vasnier, 51100 Reims. Tel: 03 26 84 43 44. Fax: 03 26 84 43 84. (M. Trezeux). Every day 0900-1145, 1400-1715; Dec-Feb closed Tue and Wed. Automated vehicle drive, with commentaries in seven languages. TP.WS.E.G.I.N. ☎ www.piper-heidsieck.com

Champagne Pommery & Greno 5, place du Général Gouraud, 51100 Reims. Tel: 03 26 61 62 56. Fax: 03 26 61 62 96. Tours: Mar-Oct, 0900-1100, 1400-1700. Oct-Mar, closed Sat, Sun and holidays. The cellars cover 18km (11 miles). TP.WS.E.G.I.S. www.pommery.fr

Champagne Ruinart 4, rue des Crayères, 51053 Reims. Tel: 03 26 77 51 51. Fax: 03 26 82 88 43. (Jennifer Mansuy). Mon-Fri 0900-1130, 1400-1630. By appointment only. Gallo-Roman cellars, a national historic monument. TF.WS.E.G.I.N. ☎ www.ruinart.com

Champagne Alain Thienot rue Joseph Cugnot, Parc d'activités, 51500 Taissy. Tel: 03 26 77 50 10. Fax: 03 26 77 50 19. By appointment only. TF.WS.E. ☎

A sign at Hautvillers, the village where Dom Perignon did so much to revolutionize the production of Champagne. The traditional bonnet protects the grape-picker from the sun.

An historic city

In some ways, the greatest moments of Reims seem to have been in the past. There still remains one of the four triumphal gates to the Roman city, the Porta Martis, which was reputedly built by Agrippa in honour of the Emperor Augustus.

For more than six centuries, the Kings of France were crowned in its Cathedral, and it was here in 1429 that Joan of Arc begged the newly crowned King Charles VII to be allowed to return to tend her flock of sheep at Domrémy.

More recently, Reims has stood in the way of a succession of invading armies from the east. In 1814, it was occupied by the Russians for twenty-four hours, before Napoleon came to recapture it in one of his last successful military operations.

In 1870, for a time it was the headquarters of the Prussian army on its way to capture Paris, and it suffered heavily from bombardment during World War I. The surrender document of the German forces was signed at what is now 12, rue Franklin Roosevelt, on 7 May 1945, to end World War II.

Reims is now an important regional centre, though being challenged as the capital of the Champagne trade by Epernay, and having lost out to Châlons-en-Champagne as the administrative centre of the *département*. It still plays an important role in the textile trade and is a major shopping centre.

From whichever direction you approach the town, it is the Cathedral that stands out. It has been described as the most perfect Gothic church building in the world. It was begun in 1212, and if the original design had been completed it would now have seven towers and spires. Nevertheless, it is still an imposing building and restoration has been sympathetically carried out.

There is some magnificent stained glass including a beautiful rose window and another designed by

Marc Chagall. The façade of the building used to feature six hundred monumental statues, but many of these were dislodged during World War I, and some can now be seen in the nearby Musée Palais du Tau.

Almost as impressive as the Cathedral is the Romanesque St.-Rémy basilica, where Saint Remigius, who brought Christianity to the Franks, is buried. Parts of it predate the Cathedral by almost 200 years. Also of interest in the town is a motor museum and, for Great War historians, there are battlefields to be visited on the doorstep.

To watch life passing by, I suggest taking a drink in one of the many open-air cafés of the Place Drouet d'Erlon.

The cellars
Of all the wines of France, it is Champagne where the brand is the most important. To support this image, many of the Champagne houses have very sophisticated facilities for welcoming visitors. The process of producing sparkling wine by the *méthode champenoise* is both complicated and time-consuming, and you should come out of the visit with a much clearer idea as to why a bottle of Champagne can be so expensive!

Whilst the cellars of Reims may be not as large as some of those of Epernay, some of them have a particular interest, in that they were originally dug in Roman times as chalk pits. Often 25 to 30 metres (80 to 90 feet) deep, they tend to be bottle-shaped, with a narrow opening at the top and widening out at the bottom. They maintain a constant temperature, ideal for the maturing of fine wines.

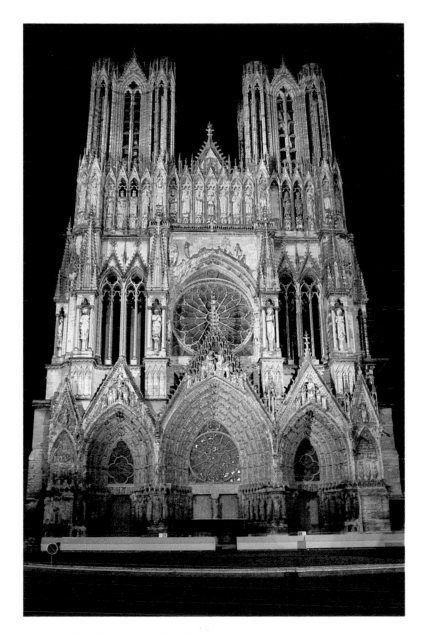

Just as in other vineyard regions, techniques are also changing in Champagne: oak casks are giving way to stainless steel, the shaking down of the sediment in the bottles is now generally controlled by a computer programme rather than by strong wrists, and the crown cork has replaced the cork stopper during the second fermentation.

A night-time view of the magnificent façade of the cathedral at Reims, where the Kings of France were traditionally crowned. The Gothic building dates back to the 13th century.

Champagne – the manufacturing process

The high reputation, and the price, of Champagne are due to a number of factors.

First of all, the vineyards are among the most northerly in the world and, as a result, it is not easy to make wine every year.

Secondly, because red grapes are largely used for making a white wine and a delicate wine at that, particular care has to be taken at the time of picking and pressing. Alone among the major vineyard regions of France, Champagne insists on the grapes being pressed as near to the vineyards as possible, rather than at the winery. Each village will have one or more press-houses.

Pressing

The pressing, too, is tightly controlled, with the grapes being pressed up to five times. The finest wines are made from the first two or three light, rapid pressings. This is known as the *cuvée*. From every four tonnes of grapes, there comes the equivalent of thirteen casks of juice. Ten of these are *cuvée*.

The second, a harder pressing, gives two casks of *première taille* juice, with the final cask coming from the *deuxième taille*. Under recent legislation, these last pressings cannot be made into Champagne.

Fermentation

The juice, or "must", from all the different villages is then brought to the cellars of the merchant for the first fermentation. When this has taken place, all the distinct wines will be blended together to produce a wine typical of the particular brand.

Bottling

The wine is then bottled, with a little sugar and wine-yeast added for the second fermentation to take place and give the sparkle to the wine. This fermentation leaves a deposit in the wine, and one of the most traditional and time-consuming stages in production takes place to prepare the bottle so that the deposit can be removed without the wine suffering. The object is to disturb the sediment gently and gradually tip the bottle so

The cellars of De Castellane Champagne at Epernay. The bottles are resting sur pointe *(upside down) with the deposit in the neck of the bottles.*

In the cellars of Champagne De Venoge, the remueur *twists the bottles to settle the deposit.*

that it is standing vertically with the neck downwards and the deposit on the cork.

The traditional way of achieving this was to put the bottles in sloping racks called *pupitres*. Every day, a specialist workman, known as a *remueur*, would give each bottle a quick twist and leave it in a slightly more vertical position. This process involved considerable labor and took several weeks. Now most companies have computer-programmed machines which achieve the same effect in a matter of days, though they keep a token number of *pupitres* for the tourists.

When the deposit has finally settled on the cork, the neck of the bottle is frozen, the cork is removed and the pressure in the bottle forces out the pellet of ice with the sediment in it. The bottle is then topped up with wine and a syrup of old wine and cane sugar, the proportion of which varies according to the degree of sweetness required in the final product. The bottle is recorked, labelled and packed, ready for dispatch.

Because of the enormous pressures involved, the bottles and the corks have to be of the finest quality.

Ageing and blending

Another contributing factor to the price paid by the customer is that most bottles of Champagne remain in the cellars for at least three years before being sold.

Most Champagnes are made from a blend of wines from the different parts of the region and from a number of different years. This enables each company to maintain continuity in style for their wines.

In the best years, however, a company might make a "vintage" wine, with a date on the label. The controls on the making of such a wine are even more strict.

Is a vintage Champagne better than a non-vintage Champagne? Not necessarily, for the ideal blend for a non-vintage wine should produce an ideally balanced wine, with the weaknesses of the wines of one year being offset by the strengths of those of another.

STYLES OF CHAMPAGNE
Apart from simple vintage and non-vintage wines, there are a number of different styles of Champagne available. Becoming increasingly fashionable is Rosé Champagne. Generally this is made by blending red and white wines before bottling. A Blanc de Blancs wine is one made exclusively from white grapes. Most of the Champagne houses also produce a de luxe *cuvée*, which generally has its own particular styled bottle.

Coteaux Champenois is the name given to the still wines of Champagne.

The Montagne de Reims and the Marne Valley

AY-CHAMPAGNE
Champagne Bollinger S.A 18 bvd du Maréchal de Lattre de Tassigny, 51160 Aÿ-Champagne. Tel: 03 26 53 33 66. Fax: 03 26 54 85 59. By appointment only. Closed Aug. E. ☎
Champagne Philipponnat 13 rue du Pont, 51160 Mareuil-sur-Aÿ. Tel: 03 26 56 93 00. Fax: 03 26 56 93 18. By appointment only. Closed Aug. WS.E. ☎ E-mail: champagne. philipponnat@wanadoo.fr
EPERNAY
Champagne Moët & Chandon *Service des Visites*, 20, ave de Champagne, 51200 Epernay. Tel: 03 26 51 20 20. Fax: 03 26 51 20 21. 1 Apr-mid Nov every day 0930-1130, 1400-1630. Rest of year Mon-Fri, same hours. TF (with entry charge). WS.E.G.I.N.S. (☎ for groups.) E-mail: ilatella@ moet.tm.fr www.moet.com

Every vineyard village of Champagne has its own classification, based on a percentage system, and it is on the basis of this rating that growers used to be paid for their grapes. At vintage time, a price per kilo of grapes would be fixed, and growers who had vineyards in a village rated at 100 per cent received the full price. Growers in a village rated at 80 per cent, the minimum rating, only received that proportion of the price.

However, price-fixing is now forbidden under EU regulations. As a result, although the village rating is maintained as a guide, growers today negotiate their prices individually with the Champagne houses.

In all, there are 17 villages with the *grand cru* status of 100 per cent, split between the Montagne de Reims, producing the red Pinot Noir grape, and the Côte de Blancs, with the white Chardonnay. There are then more than 40 *premier cru* villages rated at more than 90 per cent.

The Montagne de Reims
This lies to the south of the city of Reims, though there are some vineyards to the north-west around the village of Merfy. Surprisingly, many of the best vineyards face north – generally speaking, the best exposure to the sun is south-east. Here the dominant grape is the Pinot Noir which also produces the great red wines of Burgundy.

To join the road which winds through the wine villages of the Montagne de Reims, take the RD380 south-west out of the city in the direction of Château-Thierry. After 8km (5 miles), turn left on to the D26. This follows the vines round the foot of the hill all the way to the beginning of the Vallée de la Marne vineyards near Bouzy.

The first villages belong to what is called la Petite Montagne, and it is not until you have crossed the main N51 road that you come to the 100 per cent villages of Mailly and Verzenay, with

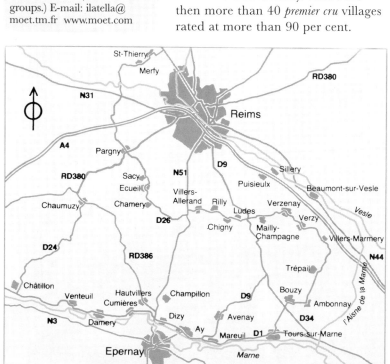

Far left: Looking across the vineyards of the Marne valley to the village of Hautvillers. In the middle distance are vineyards which have recently been replanted. It will be three years before they can produce Champagne.

Left: Hautvillers, the "Cradle of Champagne". Cumières was renowned for its red wines, and in historical times Fismes was notorious for producing "artificial" coloring wines.

its well-restored windmill. Below the road on the left lies Sillery whose wines were for long the most popular Champagnes in England. Beyond Verzenay, the direction the vineyards face changes, first towards the east and then south, where they slope down towards the river Marne. Among the great villages here is Bouzy, noted for its still, red Coteaux Champenois wine.

One of the finest views in Champagne is that of the Marne valley from the road that leads directly from Reims to Epernay. To the right is Hautvillers, with its abbey, where Dom Perignon experimented so successfully with the wines of Champagne.

Epernay

South of the Montagne de Reims is Epernay, a rather crowded, dull town, with, as its great redeeming feature, the magnificent Avenue de Champagne, flanked by some of the greatest names in the wine trade: De

Venoge and Perrier-Jouet, Mercier and Moët & Chandon.

Some of the cellars are well worth visiting. While these may not be as old as some of those of Reims, they too are cut out of the chalk, and two are so vast that they have to be visited by electric train.

The Marne Valley

Along the north bank of the river lies a great chain of vineyards stretching to the limits of the Marne *département* beyond Château Thierry thirty miles to the west of Epernay. However, almost facing Epernay are the two highest-rated villages: Aÿ and Mareuil-sur-Aÿ. The drive along this north bank is particularly attractive and provides an opportunity of visiting the Abbey of Hautvillers.

In 1822 the ruined abbey was bought by a member of the Moët family, and the company has now created a small wine museum there.

MAREUIL-LE-PORT
Champagne Comte de Lantage 20, rue de la Chapelle, Cerseuil, 51700 Mareuil-le-Port. Tel: 03 26 51 11 39. Fax: 03 26 51 11 41. (Michèle Mandois). Every day 0900-1200, 1400-1600. T.F.W.S.E.G. (☎ weekends). www.lantage.com

MERFY
Champagne Chartogne-Taillet 37-39, Grande Rue, 51220 Merfy. Tel: 03 26 03 10 17. Fax: 03 26 03 19 15. (Elisabeth Chartogne). Mon-Sat 0800-1900. Closed during vintage. Picnic area. Small family company. TF (TP for groups). W.S.E.G. ☎

TOURS-SUR-MARNE
Champagne Laurent-Perrier ave de Champagne, 51150 Tours-sur-Marne. Tel: 03 26 58 91 22. Fax: 03 26 58 77 29. (Mme Frédérique Chaise). Mon-Fri 0900-1030, 1400-1530. Closed Aug. T.F.W.S.E.G.I.S. ☎

The Côte des Blancs

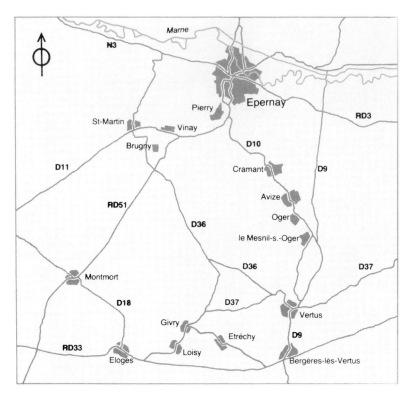

THE EXCEPTION THAT PROVES THE RULE
Champagne is the one exception to the *appellation contrôlée* rules (see page 11). The words *appellation contrôlée* never appear on the label of a bottle of Champagne, as the name Champagne in itself carries the full import of *appellation contrôlée*.

South from Epernay runs the Côte des Blancs, with the vineyards lying on easterly facing slopes below wooded hillsides. Here the other great grape of Burgundy, the Chardonnay, is grown.

The wine made from this grape adds a certain crisp delicacy to the ultimate blend, and it is not surprising in this age when lighter wines are so much appreciated that Blanc de Blancs Champagne is becoming more popular.

The road for visiting these vineyards is the D10 which branches off the main road to the south of Epernay 3 km (2 miles) from the centre of town. The two best-known village names are Cramant and Avize. The first of these used to be particularly known for its Crémant de Cramant, a wine with a much less aggressive sparkle than that usually associated with Champagne. However, the term *Crémant* is no longer permitted for Champagne, and is now reserved for sparkling wine from other regions, such as *Crémant d'Alsace* and *Crémant de Loire*.

The vineyards of the Côte des Blancs finish just beyond the village of Vertus, where there is a most impressive church, with a spring beneath it. Just 5 km (3 miles) further south, a good view back over the vineyards can be had from the top of Mont Saint Aimé, where there are the ruins of an old château.

Southern Champagne vineyards

Although the heart of the Champagne vineyards could be said to finish here, there are three substantial enclaves of vines to the south with every right to the name Champagne. Much of the wine disappears into the blends of the big brands of Reims and Epernay and it is only recently that some of the local growers have begun to make efforts to sell their wines under their own labels.

These vineyards are historical relics of the territories of the Count of Champagne, and indeed at their southern extremity they approach the northern limits of the vineyards of Burgundy.

Of the three vineyard areas, the first, the Côte de Sézanne, is still in the Marne *département* and is effectively a continuation of the Côte des Blancs. The other two areas are in the *département* of the Aube and for many years had to label their wines in a pejorative way as Champagne Deuxième Zone. They are Bar-sur-Aude and Bar-sur-Seine. Just outside the former are the remains of what

BAR-SUR-SEINE
**Champagne Veuve A.
Devaux** Domaine de
Villeneuve, 10110 Bar-Sur-
Seine. Tel: 03 25 38 30 65.
Fax: 03 25 29 73 21. (M.
Paul Baniol). Mon-Fri
0800-1200, 1330-1730.
Closed Aug. T.F.WS.E. ☎
E-mail: champagnedevaux@
wanadoo.fr
LES RICEYS
**Champagne Alexandre
Bonnet** 10340 Les Riceys.
Tel: 03 25 29 30 93.
Fax: 03 25 29 38 65.
(M. Gérard Rafai). Mon-
Fri 0800-1200, 1400-1800.
Champagne, Coteaux
Champenois red, Rosé des
Riceys. T.F.WS.E.
URVILLE
Champagne Drappier
Grande Rue, 10200
Urville. Tel: 03 26 05 13 01.
Fax: 03 25 27 41 19. (Michel
Drappier). Mon-Sat 0800-
1200, 1400-1800. Cellars
dating from 12th century.
T.F.WS.E.G. ☎
E-mail: champagnedrappier@
wanadoo.fr
www.champagne-multimedia.
com/drappier
FOR FURTHER INFORMATION
C.I.V.C. 5, Rue Henri
Martin, 51204 Epernay.
Tel: 03 26 51 19 30. Fax:
03 26 55 19 79. G.N.S.
www.champagne.fr

used to be a Roman camp on the summit of the Colline Sainte-Germaine. This site had two great advantages: not only was it easily defended, but it was well watered by a spring.

Apart from their sparkling wines, the vineyards of Bar-sur-Seine are noted for a still wine with its own *appellation*, Les Riceys. This is most often a rosé, but occasionally a red wine made from the Pinot Noir grape, and comes much closer to the

The Côte des Blancs stretching south from Epernay where only the Chardonnay is grown. This grape is used to make Blanc de Blancs Champagne, where no red grapes are used.

wine of Burgundy than anything else that one might find in Champagne.

The wine roads in the main part of the Champagne vineyards are well signposted and there are separate routes for the Montagne de Reims, the Vallée de la Marne and the Côte des Blancs.

Alsace

GRAND CRU APPELLATION
In 1975, as part of a continuous quality improvement programme, the Alsace growers established a *Grand Cru appellation*. This is based on the soil and aspect to the sun of individual vineyards. Yields in such vineyards are limited to not more than 65 hl/ha (less than four tonnes an acre), and vines are restricted to "the four noble grapes" – Riesling, Muscat, Gewürztraminer and Pinot Gris. Ninety-three sites were originally considered for possible *Grand Cru* status. Twenty-five of these were selected in 1983, and this figure has since grown to 50.

WINE MUSEUM
Château de Kientzheim, Kientzheim, 68240
Tel: 03 89 78 21 36.
Every day 1000-1200, 1400-1800.

WINE FESTIVALS
The festival season starts on 1 May and ends in late Oct; the peak period is July and Aug. In all, there are approximately 45 festivals each year. The main one is the regional wine fair at Colmar, 1st. fortnight in Aug. A full list is available from C.I.V.A. address below.

FOR FURTHER INFORMATION
C.I.V.A. Maison des Vins d'Alsace, 12, ave de la Foire-aux-Vins, 68012 Colmar. Tel: 03 89 20 16 20. Fax: 03 89 20 16 30.
E-mail: c.i.v.a.@rmcnet.fr

Through the centuries, Alsace has been the bone over which France and Germany have fought. It is only since the end of World War I that it has been definitively French; indeed some of the older men fought in the German army. As a result the area has a happy blend of styles, in the architecture, in the food and in the wine. However, the growers that you will meet are proud that they are neither French nor German: they are *Alsacien*.

With the Vosges mountains as a backdrop the vineyards of Alsace are among the prettiest in France, and those villages that have not suffered in the succession of Franco-German wars are picture-postcard material. Strasbourg and Colmar are two beautiful towns with imposing buildings and museums. Of all the vineyard regions of France, Alsace is, in many ways, the most satisfying to visit.

The dominant feature on any Alsace wine label is likely to be not the name of a village or a vineyard, but rather a grape variety. Here wines are normally made from one of seven different grapes.

Each of these seven has its own characteristics. Only one, the Pinot Noir, gives a red, or more often a deep, refreshing, fruity rosé wine.

Two of the white grapes, the Sylvaner and the Pinot Blanc (or Clevner), give wines for everyday drinking. The Sylvaner, found more in the Bas-Rhin, the northerly end of the vineyards, gives a rather full, earthy wine while the Pinot Blanc makes a lighter, crisp style, and is often used in making the local AOC sparkling wine, the Crémant d'Alsace.

The four noble grapes
The four noble grapes are the Pinot Gris, known also as the Tokay Pinot Gris, the Gewurztraminer, the Muscat and the Riesling. The Pinot Gris is full, soft and supple, often high in alcohol.

The Muscat and the Gewurztraminer both give very full-flavored wine. The Muscat comes from the same grape as many of the great sweet dessert wines of the world.

The spire of the Cathedral at Strasbourg, which was completed in 1439. It towers some 143 metres (469 feet) above the historic heart of the cité.

This has a similar taste, but is dry. The Gewurztraminer's spicy flavor reminds me of Ogen melons (one of the cantaloup varieties).

Alsace growers are proudest of their Rieslings. At their best, these are classic, steely, austere wines, whose flavor seems to remain in your mouth for ever.

All these wines are dry, but, in the greatest years, sweeter wines are sometimes made from late-picked grapes. The label will then say *Vendange Tardive*, or for the very finest and most expensive wines, *Sélection de Grains Nobles*. These last rate with the finest Sauternes.

To get to Alsace
Colmar is 444km (277 miles) E of Paris – by N4 to Luneville, then N59 and N415; 557km (348 miles) by A4 motorway to Strasbourg, then N83; 683km (426 miles) from Calais via Reims; 290km (181 miles) by A36 from Beaune.

Bas-Rhin

Haut-Rhin

The Wine Route

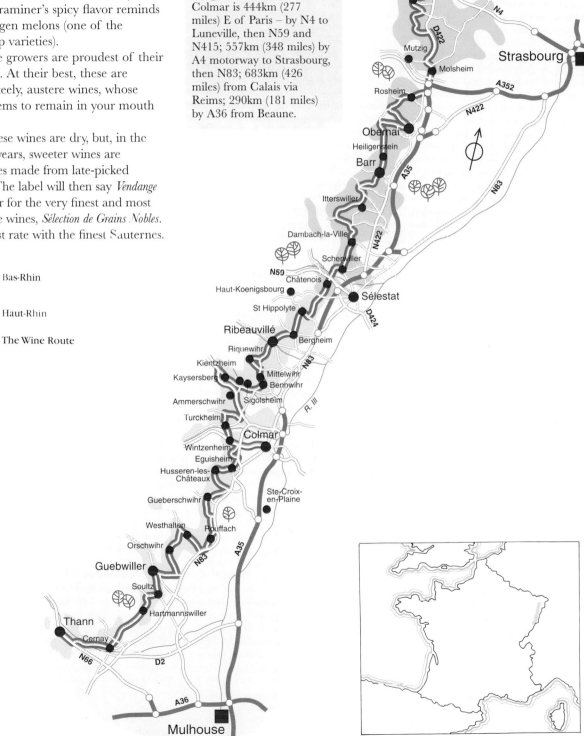

27

The Bas-Rhin

BARR

Alsace Willm S.A. 32, rue du Dr Sulzer, 67140 Barr. Tel: 03 88 08 19 11. Fax: 03 88 08 56 21. (Mme Heym). Mon-Fri 0830-1200, 1400-1700. TF.WS.E.G. ☎ E-mail: alsace-willm@ wanadoo.fr www.alsace-willm.com

Domaine Klipfel 6 ave de la Gare, 67140 Barr. Tel: 03 88 58 59 00. Fax: 03 88 08 53 18. (Mme Lorentz or Mme Müller). Every day 1000-1200, 1400-1800. Closed Jan. Guided tour, video, museum. TP.WS. ☎ E-mail: alsace-wine@ klipfel.com

MITTELBERGHEIM

Maison Pierre et Albert Seltz S.A.R.L. 21, rue Principale, 67140 Mittelbergheim. Tel: 03 88 08 91 77. Fax: 03 88 08 52 72. (M. Seltz). Mon-Fri 0800-1200, 1400-1800. TP.WS.E.

WISSEMBOURG

Cave Viticole de Cleebourg 67160 Wissembourg. Tel: 03 88 94 50 33. Fax: 03 88 94 57 08. (Mme Schab). Mon-Sat 0800-1200, 1400-1800; Sun, holidays 1000-1200, 1400-1800. Closed Christmas, New Year and Easter. TF (TP for large groups). WS.E.G. ☎ E-mail: cave.cleebourg@ wanadoo.fr

The Château of Haut-Koenigsbourg, which despite its appearance was built at the beginning of this century by Kaiser Wilhelm II, when Alsace formed part of Germany.

Although the main Alsace wine road starts at Marlenheim to the west of Strasbourg, there is a small enclave of vines near Wissembourg, some 60 km (38 miles) to the north.

There is an interesting contrast between the host of vines on the German side of the frontier and the few on the French, where all the grapes are sent to the pretty little Co-operative Cellar at Cleebourg.

On the drive up to Wissembourg, the pottery villages of Soufflenheim and Betschdorf, the Forest of Haguenau and such charming half-timbered farming villages as Oberseebach and Niederseebach are worth a visit.

Strasbourg

While Strasbourg itself is away from the vineyard area, the wine-lover can justify a visit there for its numerous *winstuben*, or wine taverns. These play an important part in the daily life of Alsace and are ideal places in which to taste a range of wines by the glass or bottle and to eat the local gastronomic specialties at a reasonable price.

For the architecturally minded, the cathedral and the old quarter of the city have to be visited.

To reach the wine road from Strasbourg, take the main N4 road west and, after 20km (12.5 miles), you come to Marlenheim. It is here that the main vineyards of Alsace begin.

The vinous reputation of Marlenheim is based on its red, or more properly rosé wine. From Marlenheim, the *Route des Vins* is clearly marked, as it meanders its way south. For the first few miles, names will strike a chord probably more with beer drinkers than with wine drinkers as one drives through the village of Mützig and passes the modern Kronenbourg brewery.

Villages of the Bas-Rhin

Rosheim still has fortified gateways dating back to the 14th century. If only to get a good view of the vineyards and the plain of the Bas-Rhin, visit the Mont Sainte Odile, above Obernai. Here are the remains of an abbey and a convent to the memory of this 7th-century saint.

Obernai is an attractive town with a beautiful market-place and 16th-century well. Between Obernai and the next town, Barr, comes a succession of pretty villages tucked into the feet of the Vosges mountains. Of these, I can recommend Ottrott as a local base. Heiligenstein even has its own grape variety, the Clevner de Heiligenstein, a type of Gewurztraminer.

Barr is a centre of the tanning industry as well as the wine-trade. It has an important wine fair each July and is particularly proud of its Gewurztraminer wines.

Just to the south comes Mittelbergheim, where the best Sylvaners are made, and Dambach, which has more vineyards than any other village in Alsace. If you look at the coat of arms of the village, you will see that the dominant feature is a bear.

The story has it that a young child once strayed away from the village and came across a wild bear eating mouthfuls of berries. The child was so amazed that he took some home to his parents – and thus the merits of grapes were discovered.

At the southern extremity of the Bas-Rhin *département*, on a crest of the Vosges, is the remarkable Château du Haut-Koenigsbourg. The ideal location for any Dracula film, this castle was built by Kaiser Wilhelm II, at the beginning of this century, on the ruins of a Swiss feudal stronghold. The winding road up to it gives some sensational views. Just to the north, there is an interesting excursion up the valley of the Giessen. This is the centre for the distillation of the white spirits for which Alsace is noted.

Traditional Alsace architecture in the town of Barr. The word winstub *means a bar serving local wines by the bottle or glass.*

The Haut-Rhin

AMMERSCHWIHR
Domaine Sick-Dreyer
17, rte de Kientzheim,
68770 Ammerschwihr. Tel:
03 89 47 11 31. Fax:
03 89 47 32 60. (M. or
Mme Pierre Dreyer). Mon-
Sat 0800-1200, 1330-1800.
Closed Sun. TF (with
purchase of wine) WS.E.G.
(☎ at weekends).
Email: edreyer@wanadoo.fr
www.sick-dreyer.com

BEBLENHEIM
Cave Vinicole
14, rue de Hoen, 68980
Beblenheim. Tel:
03 89 47 90 02. Fax:
03 89 47 86 85. (Mme
Anne-Laure Morat). Every
day 0800-1200, 1400-1730.
TP.WS.E.G.☎

BENNWIHR
Bestheim 3, rue du Général
de Gaulle, 68630 Bennwihr.
Tel: 03 89 49 09 29. Fax:
03 89 49 09 20. Every day
0900-1200, 1400-1800.
Closed Christmas.
TF.WS.E.G.

There is no great difference in the
scenery between the Haut-Rhin and
the Bas-Rhin, but for the wine-lover
there is a world of difference in the
quality of the wines. With a few
notable exceptions, all the great
wines of Alsace come from the
southern end of the vineyards.

Ribeauvillé
The first wine village in the Haut-
Rhin is Saint-Hyppolyte, which, like
Marlenheim, is known for its red

*The colorful façade of a house at Riquewihr, one of
France's most beautiful wine-villages. Many cellars
here are open for wine tasting.*

wines, but the first of the great
villages is Ribeauvillé. Perhaps the
finest Riesling of Alsace, the Clos
Saint Hune, comes from here and,
to balance it out, there is an
important bottling plant for mineral
water.

The last Sunday in August is
known here as the *Pfifferday*, or
Piper's Day. Each year there are
colorful festivities, with free wine
flowing in the Town Hall Square.

Just south of the village, at
Hunawihr, efforts have been made to
reintroduce the stork – the bird for
which the region is best known.
Storks can be seen here during the
nesting season.

Riquewihr
Just 4 km (2.5 miles) to the south
comes Riquewihr, which must be one
of the most beautiful wine villages in
the world. In an area which has
suffered regularly from the ravages of
war, somehow Riquewihr has
managed to escape, and it remains to
this day a 16th-century fortified
village.

The best time to visit must be in
October during the vintage, for
many of the cellars of both growers
and merchants are on the main
street, the rue du Général de Gaulle.
To refresh yourself, some of the
growers have *winstuben*, where the
traditional way of taking the new
wine is with walnuts and fresh bread.

As an alternative diversion, there
is also a museum of postal history.

If Riquewihr has escaped damage
in succeeding wars, the same cannot
be said for the neighbouring twin
villages of Mittelwihr and Bennwihr.
They were the scene of some of the
fiercest fighting during World War II,
and were almost totally destroyed.

A girl in traditional costume poses in Kaysersberg, where Albert Schweitzer was born. Here, many of the houses date back 500 years.

They have now been rebuilt in traditional Alsace style.

The Weiss Valley

Shortly after these two villages, the *Route des Vins* turns off to the right up the valley of the Weiss. The first village, Sigolsheim, was also destroyed in World War II, but Kientzheim still has a fortified gateway, with a sculpture of a man's head putting out his tongue at any assailant, and a château, which is the base of the *Confrérie Saint-Etienne*, the local drinking brotherhood. Here they hold their regular banquets and maintain a wine museum.

To the left of the road between Kientzheim and the next village, Kaysersberg, lies the Weinbach, a wine estate that used to belong to a Capuchin convent.

Kaysersberg

Kaysersberg's name, "Caesar's Hill", goes back to Roman times, when it guarded the end of the most strategic pass between Gaul and the plains of Alsace. Many of the buildings that remain date back to the 15th and 16th centuries, including a fortified bridge with a chapel on it. It is the proud birthplace of Albert Schweitzer.

In Kaysersberg, the wine road again turns back on itself, down the N415, through the important wine village of Ammerschwihr, to the centre of the wine-trade of Alsace, Colmar.

Colmar

This attractive town, with its fine medieval centre, is a good base for the wine tourist. The regional wine fair takes place in August, in the exhibition hall to the north of the town. There is no better occasion on which to taste a full range of wines from throughout the region.

KIENTZHEIM
Paul Blanck et Fils
32, Grand'Rue, 68240 Kientzheim. Tel: 03 89 78 23 56. Fax: 03 89 47 16 45. Mon-Sat 0900-1200, 1300-1830. T.F.WS.E.G. E-mail: blanck-alsace@ rmcnet.fr www.blanck.com

RIQUEWIHR
Daniel Wiederhirn
7, rue du Cheval, 68340 Riquewihr. Tel: 03 89 47 92 10. Fax: 03 89 49 06 45. 1100-1200, 1300-1330, 1800-2000. Small grower's cellars from 16th century. TF (with purchase of wine). WS.G.

Dopff "au Moulin"
68340 Riquewihr. Tel: 03 89 49 09 69. Fax: 03 89 47 83 61. (M. Herold). Apr-Nov every day 0900-1200, 1400-1800. Still and sparkling wines. T.F.WS.E.G. (TP ☎ for groups.) www.dopff-au-moulin.fr

Hugel et Fils S.A.
3, rue de la 1ère Armée Française, 68340 Riquewihr. Tel: 03 89 47 92 15. Fax: 03 89 49 00 10. (Etienne Hugel or David Ling). Mon-Thur 0800-1200, 1330-1730, Fri 0800-1200. Closed weekends, first two weeks Aug and vintage time. Historic cellars, including oldest wine cask still in use in the world. Tasting shop 1000-1200, 1400-1800 daily. T.F.WS.E.G. ☎ E-mail: hugel1639@wanadoo.fr www.hugel.com

EGUISHEIM
Vins Wolfberger Cave Vinicole Eguisheim, 6, Grand' Rue, 68420 Eguisheim. Tel: 03 89 22 20 20. Fax: 03 89 23 47 09. (Yves Lithard or Annette Kempf). Mon-Sat 0800-1200, 1400-1800, Sun 1000-1200, 1400-1800. TP.WS. (E in week only). E-mail: wolfberger@ wanadoo.fr

GUEBWILLER
Domaines Schlumberger
100, rue Theodore Deck, 68501 Guebwiller. Tel: 03 89 74 27 00. Fax: 03 89 74 85 75. Mon-Fri 0800-1200, 1400-1700. Closed 1-15 Aug. T.F.WS.E.G. ☎
E-mail: duschlum@aol.com

HUSSEREN-LES-CHATEAUX
Vins Kuentz-Bas 14, rte du Vin, 68420 Husseren-les-Châteaux. Tel: 03 89 49 30 24. Fax: 03 89 49 23 39. (Christian or Jean-Michel Bas). Mon-Fri 0900-1200, 1300-1800. Sat by appointment only. Closed Sun. T.F.WS.E.G. ☎
www.kuentz-bas.fr

ROUFFACH
Vignobles Muré Clos St. Landelin, RN83, 68250 Rouffach. Tel: 03 89 78 58 00. Fax: 03 89 78 58 01. Mon-Sat 0800-1700. T.F.WS.E.G.
www.mure.com

Alsace is a region of fine food – here is a display of a local baker's work. On the right are two of the local Kugelhopf *cakes.*

Colmar is an ideal base for visiting the vineyards of Alsace. It is also very beautiful in its own right. Well worth visiting are the old quarter, with its network of canals, and the Musée d'Unterlinden.

A chain of villages
While Colmar may make a convenient break in the Alsace wine road, the hardy traveller will cut across from Ammerschwihr to the walled village of Turckheim, where, every evening in summer, the nightwatchman, with halberd and lantern in hand, walks round telling all the inhabitants to go to bed.

Eguisheim
Eguisheim is another in the chain of beautiful Alsace villages. Its cobbled streets are alight with flowers and even its co-operative cellar, the largest in Alsace, blends into the general picture. The village's most famous son is Pope Leo IX, who was

Supreme Pontiff during the middle of the 11th century.

Above Eguisheim, half-way up the hillside, lies Husseren-les-Châteaux, itself dominated by the ruins of three castles on the Vosges skyline.

Rouffach
The wine villages continue in a chain on the slopes above the fast-moving traffic of the N83. This skirts the pretty village of Rouffach, whose wines were described a quarter of a century ago as having a "spiritual" bouquet.

One of its vineyards, the Clos St.-Landelin, has a microclimate that is claimed to be the driest in all of France. (St. Landelin was an itinerant Irish monk who came to convert the Germans during the 4th century and founded a monastery, just across the Rhine, in the Black Forest in Germany.)

Guebwiller
Of all the Alsace wine-towns, Guebwiller must be the least attractive. It owes its size, and its wealth, to the textile machinery factories of the Schlumbergers. Since the time of the French Revolution this family has built up what is now the largest single wine domain in Alsace – and the largest

single hillside wine property in France.

This now extends to 140 hectares (340 acres), spread along south-facing slopes overlooking the town. It is so steep in places that tractors are unable to work the vines and a team of twelve horses is still kept for the purpose (and for a natural supply of manure).

The end of the wine road

Towards its southern end the *Route des Vins* seems to lose its purpose for a while, as the vineyards become fewer and the landscape becomes dominated by the potash mines in the plain. However it comes to a glorious finale with the Rangen vineyard, of volcanic soil, overlooking the town of Thann.

Most of the wine villages of Alsace that the traveller may wish to visit lie in a narrow strip along the flanks of the Vosges, and there is no easy circuit that can be made. Nevertheless, because of their wines, their beauty and their hospitality, even the shortest visit to any part of them is always rewarding.

A land of plenty

Well endowed with agricultural and natural resources, Alsace has its own distinctive regional cuisine. This can call upon fish from the tributaries of the Rhine, as well as game from the Vosges forests. The food is a hearty blend of much that is best from the cooking of both France and Germany. As a local saying has it, "The Frenchman likes to eat well, the German likes to eat a lot, the Alsacien likes to eat well – and a lot."

For those wishing to try the local wines, and not wanting to eat too

In the Riquewihr cellars of grower and merchant Hugel is the oldest wine-cask in the world still in use. Called the Sainte Catherine, it was constructed in 1715. (Particulars of the company will be found on page 31.)

heavily, *winstuben* (wine taverns) serve simple dishes and wines by the glass as well as the bottle.

With fine food and wine at fair prices, Alsace is a happy hunting-ground for the thrifty gastronome.

WINTZENHEIM
Vins Josmeyer 76, rue Clemenceau, 68920 Wintzenheim. Tel: 03 89 27 91 90. Fax: 03 89 27 91 99. (M. Christophe Ehrhart or M. Jean Meyer). Mon-Fri 0900-1130, 1400-1700, Sat 0900-1130. Closed Sun and holidays. TF (TP for groups).WS.E.G. www.josmeyer.com

Burgundy

FOR FURTHER INFORMATION
B.I.V.B. 12, bvd
Bretonnière, B.P. 150, 21204
Beaune. Tel: 03 80 25 04 80.
Fax: 03 80 25 04 81.
TP.E.☎ E-mail: bivb@
wanadoo.fr www.bivb.com

Vintage time in Burgundy. Grape-picking in the Beaujolais with the hill of Brouilly in the background. The tractor is specially designed to drive over the rows of vines.

If there is one vineyard region in France that has the image of living life to the full, it must be Burgundy. Whether it fully lives up to this role is for the visitor to decide, but there is no doubt that it is a land of robust wine and hearty food. For the Burgundian, nouvelle cuisine only exists in fairyland, and not the land of good fairies, at that.

Burgundians are proud of their history; once their Dukes ruled territory that stretched as far as what is now Belgium. They are proud, too, of their wines and it is this pride that makes them happy to show them off and talk about them to every visitor who shows a genuine interest. Burgundy has a reputation not just for its food and wine, but also for its hospitality.

The vineyards of Burgundy are shared between four different *départements*: the Yonne, Côte d'Or, Saône et Loire and the Rhône – and between five separate and largely distinct regions: Chablis and the Auxerrois, the Côte d'Or, the Côte Chalonnaise, the Mâconnais and the Beaujolais.

While the reputations of the wines of Burgundy and Bordeaux may be on a par, in an average vintage Bordeaux produces two and a half times as much wine. Another interesting comparison is to consider the total production of Burgundy to be one bottle of wine. Out of that bottle, just one glassful comes from the Yonne and the Côte d'Or – those vineyards from which are made the wines that have made the reputation of Burgundy: Chablis and Meursault; Nuits-Saint-Georges and Beaune; Pommard and Gevrey-Chambertin.

By far the bulk of the production comes from the vineyards of the Beaujolais and the Mâconnais. It is because of this small production that

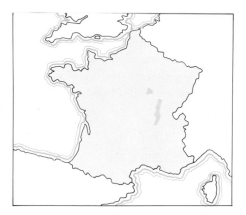

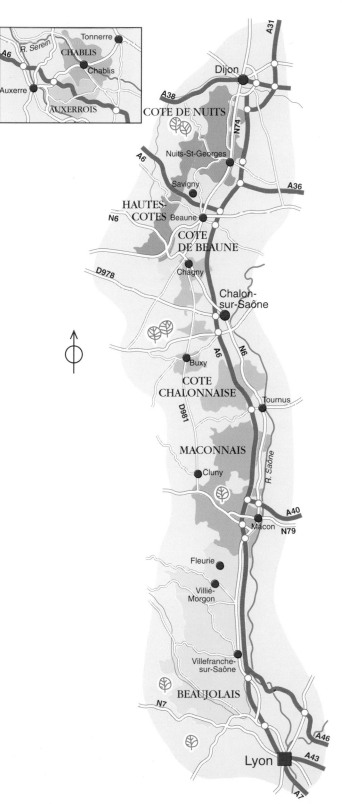

To get to Burgundy
Chablis is 181km (113 miles) from Paris by motorway (A6, exit at Auxerre Sud), Beaune is 312km (195 miles) from Paris. Chablis is 186km (116 miles) from Reims by the A4, A26, N77 and D91. Beaune is 261km (163 miles) from Colmar by the N83 and A36 and 600km (373 miles) from Calais by motorway.

the great wines of Burgundy are never cheap. It must also be said that eating in Burgundy is not cheap either, particularly if you want a well-known named wine with your meal.

A voyage of discovery
Here, then, is one of the attractions of the region: seeking out the lesser-known wines and the good restaurants off the beaten track. There are fine discoveries to be made in the small villages away from the main roads.

The expansion in the number of hotel rooms in such towns as Beaune and Nuits-Saint-Georges bears witness to their popularity as tourist centers. I would suggest that you see there what has to be seen, but there is much else besides in Burgundy.

Chablis

BEINES
**Domaine Alain
Geoffroy** 4, rue de
l'équerre, Beines, 89800
Chablis. Tel: 03 86 42 43 76.
Fax: 03 86 42 13 30. Every
day 0800-1200, 1400-1800.
TF.WS.E.
CHABLIS
Domaine Vocoret et Fils
40 rte d'Auxerre, 89800
Chablis. Tel: 03 86 42 12 53.
Fax: 03 86 42 10 39. (Mme.
Patrice and Jerome Vocoret).
Mon-Sat 0800-1200, 1330-
1730. TF. (TP for groups.) WS.
www.vocoret.com
La Chablisienne 8, bvd
Pasteur, 89800 Chablis.
Tel: 03 86 42 89 89. Fax:
03 86 42 89 90. Mon-Sat
0900-1200, 1400-1800;
Sun and holidays 0930-
1200, 1400-1800. TF. (TP.
☎ for groups) WS.E.
www.chablisienne.com

When you first see the small town of
Chablis, there is a certain feeling of
anti-climax. It seems surprising that
such a little place should have become
synonymous throughout the world
with dry white wine. While there may
still be vast quantities of so-called
Chablis produced in California, the
real thing comes from just here, and a
few surrounding villages.

Renaissance of Chablis

Historically, the reputation of Chablis
was based on communications, for
the wines could simply be shipped
downstream to the ever-thirsty
market of Paris. However, the soil is
poor and the climate severe, so when
the added burden of the *phylloxera*
plague arrived at the end of the last
century, many of the vineyards were
simply abandoned and allowed to
return to scrub. It is only during
the past twenty years or so, when
increased demand and improved
techniques have made replanting
profitable, that the true renaissance in
Chablis has occurred.

Classification

There is a rigid hierarchy in the
classification of the wines of Chablis.
At the top come the seven *grand cru*
vineyards, and these lie together on
one slope just a few hundred meters
to the north of the town, across the
river Serein.

From left to right, as you face the
hillside, they are Bougros, Les
Preuses, Vaudésir, Grenouilles,
Valmur, Les Clos (the largest and my
favorite) and Blanchots.

Next there come a host of *premiers
crus*. These lie on southerly facing
slopes on both sides of the river and
of the small valleys that run off it.
Perhaps the best-known *premier cru*
wines are Montée de Tonnerre
Fourchaume, Vaillons and
Montmains.

Ordinary Chablis comes from a
number of small surrounding villages,
where the stony soil is a limestone
based on shells that predate human
habitation.

Finally comes Petit Chablis, made
in declining quantities in villages on
the fringe of the area.

Recent changes

As replanting has taken place the
area under vines and the total crop
have increased considerably over the
recent past, more than ten times in
the past forty years and four times in
the last twenty.

The grand cru *vineyards of Chablis all lie on one
hillside behind the town. These vines are at Vaudésir.*

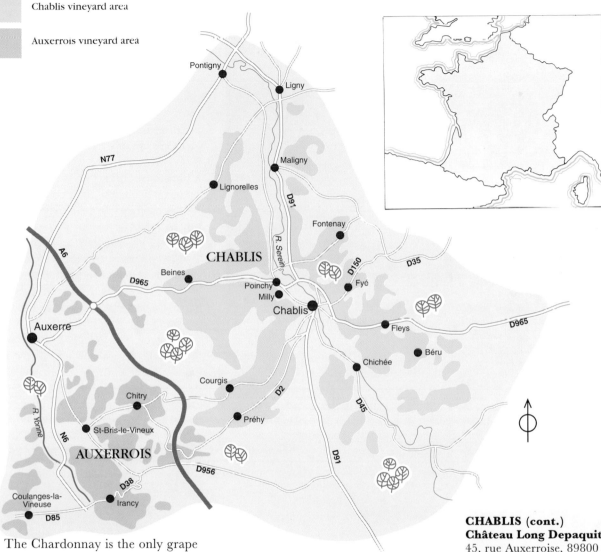

Chablis vineyard area

Auxerrois vineyard area

The Chardonnay is the only grape allowed for making the wines of Chablis, and it gives a steely, dry wine that is the ideal match for shellfish.

Over the past few years, the style of the wines of Chablis has gently altered, perhaps as a result of the demands of the market. True austerity seems to be something of the past. Nowadays a degree of softness is often present.

The town of Chablis

Despite the fact that during the last war it suffered as a result of an extempore air raid from the Italian air force, much of old Chablis survives. There are a number of houses dating back to the 14th and 15th centuries, and the Porte Noël, which was rebuilt in 1770.

At the end of a series of narrow streets, the door of the parish church, begun in the 13th century, is covered with horseshoes. These are offerings to Saint Martin, the patron saint of horsemen and all things equestrian.

CHABLIS (cont.)
Château Long Depaquit
45, rue Auxerroise, 89800 Chablis. Tel: 03 86 42 11 13. Fax: 03 86 42 81 89. (M. Gérard Vullien). Every day 0900-1830, open all year. TF.WS.E. (☎ for groups.)

WINE FESTIVALS
Les Pastorales Chablisiennes
First weekend in May.
Chablis Wine Festival
Fourth weekend in Nov.

FOR FURTHER INFORMATION
B.I.V.B. Le Petit Pontigny, 1, rue de Chichée, 89800 Chablis. Tel: 03 86 42 42 22. Fax: 03 86 42 80 16.

37

The Yonne

A traditional grower's cellar in the village of Irancy, noted for its full-bodied red wines. Here, the cellars are deep underneath the houses on both sides of the main street.

Historically, the Yonne Valley was the part of Burgundy with the greatest number of vineyards. A combination of the extreme climate, *phylloxera*, the coming of the railway (enabling wines to be brought to Paris cheaply from the vineyards of the south of France) as well as the increasing availability of other forms of employment, led to their being almost totally abandoned, apart from a hard core at Chablis.

Now, there is a renaissance in the wines of the Yonne, and not just in the wines of Chablis. While there are about 4000 hectares (9680 acres) of Chablis vineyards, there are a further 1000 hectares of vineyards producing a variety of other wines. The viability of these new vineyards is largely underwritten by "farm-gate sales" to the hordes of Parisians who descend on the region every weekend seeking to replenish their wine-cellars.

Crémant de Bourgogne
Perhaps the most exciting development has taken place in a former quarry and in the mushroom cellars in the village of Bailly on the banks of the river Yonne, just off the N6, south of Auxerre. Here, in 1972, 80 growers banded together to form a company to produce sparkling Crémant de Bourgogne. With a stock of some four million bottles and an average of two thousand visitors a week this has now become a very large scale operation.

A local specialty
Up a steep, narrow road behind Bailly lies the mother village of Saint-Bris-le-Vineux, which is by far the most important vineyard village in the Yonne *département*, outside the Chablis vineyards. The streets are full of growers' houses, with beneath them narrow, deep cellars. Many of the growers make wines from the Chardonnay and Aligoté grapes, but there is also a local specialty, the Sauvignon de Saint-Bris. This is the only place in Burgundy where this grape is grown, and it gives a wine that is similar in style to Sancerre.

Just 4km (2.5 miles) away is the village of Chitry-le-Fort, renowned for its Bourgogne Aligoté. Here there is a fortified church dating back to the 13th century.

The vineyards of Irancy are intermingled with cherry orchards and they produce a full-bodied red wine from the Pinot Noir and the César, a traditional local grape. The soil is very similar to that of Chablis, and oyster fossils can be picked up everywhere. The vines are in a natural amphitheater, which is a sun-trap. The vineyard with the highest reputation is la Palote.

On the west bank of the river Yonne lie two vineyard villages, Coulanges-la-Vineuse and Vaux. At Coulanges a softer red wine is made from the Pinot Noir and at Vaux there is the charmingly named vineyard of Dessus-Bon-Boire, which, loosely translated, means "above good drinking!"

Auxerre

The most important town in the region is Auxerre, which has a very pretty old quarter and the Gothic cathedral of Saint Stephen. There is also a 15th-century clock tower, with not only a sundial, but also a moondial.

Of the formerly famous vineyards of Auxerre, there is only one survivor, the Clos de la Chaînette, which is run by the local psychiatric hospital and which produces agreeable Bourgogne blanc and rosé.

It is worth mentioning two historic vineyards that have now been reconstituted. The first is the south-facing Côte Saint Jacques, which overlooks the town of Joigny. Here most of the wine made is a *vin gris*, or pale rosé, from the Pinot Noir and Pinot Gris.

In the second example, visitors to the splendid church built to honor the remains of St.-Mary-Magdalene at Vézelay can now once again taste the local wine, for some of the local growers have joined together to plant some 20 hectares (50 acres) of vines to make both red and white wine.

Looking down on the village of Irancy from the vineyards. As well as producing wine, the village has a high reputation for its cherries. Many of the local people own both orchards and vines.

IRANCY
Robert Colinot Irancy, 89290 Champs sur Yonne. Tel: 03 86 42 20 76. (Mme Rosa Colinot). By appointment only. TF.WS. ☎

ST.-BRIS-LE-VINEUX
Sicava, Caves de Bailly 89530 St.-Bris-le-Vineux. Tel: 03 86 53 77 77. Fax: 03 86 53 80 94. Mon-Fri 0800-1200, 1400-1800. Sat, Sun 1000-1200, 1430-1800. Apr-Sep, guided tour (one hour) 1430-1700. Free glass and tasting of sparkling wines and liqueurs. TP.WS.E.G. ☎

WINE MUSEUM
89580 Coulanges-la-Vineuse. Tel: 03 86 42 20 59. Guided tour. ☎

WINE FESTIVALS
Chablis Festival, fourth weekend in Nov.
Coulanges-la-Vineuse Festival of St. Vincent, Sun nearest 22 Jan.
Joigny Vintage Festival, last Sun in Oct.
St.-Bris-le-Vineux Sauvignon Festival, second weekend in Nov.

Sancerre and Pouilly-sur-Loire

While it may seem strange to include the vineyards of Sancerre and Pouilly-sur-Loire in the section on Burgundy, there is some logic in it, for Pouilly lies administratively within the region of Burgundy and the main vineyards of the Loire are twice as far away as those of Chablis.

Sancerre – the town

The town of Sancerre lies on a hill dominating the left bank of the river Loire. Its strategic importance has long been recognized, and some believe that it is the Cortona of Caesar's *Commentaries*. The château now belongs to the Marnier-Lapostolle family, major local vineyard owners, one of whose ancestors created the Grand Marnier liqueur.

Sancerre – the wines

Sancerre is known mainly for its white wine made from the Sauvignon grape. It is perhaps in Sancerre that the Sauvignon best shows its characteristics,

The village of Sancerre is dominated by its château. Fine wines are made here from the Sauvignon grape.

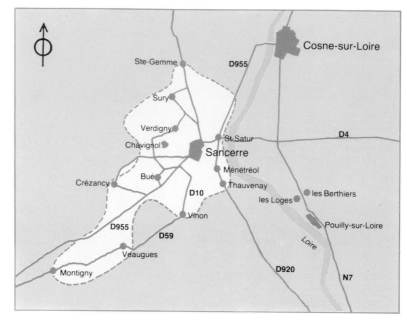

with a green stalkiness that you either love or hate. However an increasing quantity of red and rosé wine is now being made from the Pinot Noir.

The wines are produced in Sancerre itself and 13 other surrounding villages. As far as reputation is concerned, perhaps the most important is Bué. Here the best-

SANCERRE
Henri Bourgeois
Chavignol, 18300 Sancerre.
Tel: 00 48 78 53 20.
Fax: 02 48 54 14 24.
Caves de la Mignonne
18300 Sancerre. Tel: 02 48 54 07 06. Fax: 02 48 78 51 04. 15 Mar-15 Nov only, every day 0930-1200, 1430-1900. TP.WS.
Gitton Père et Fils
Chemin de Lavaud, Menetréol sous Sancerre, 18300 Sancerre. Tel: 02 48 54 38 84. Fax: 02 48 54 09 59. (M. Gitton). Mon-Fri 0900-1200, 1400-1800 (1700 Fri). Sat, Sun by appointment only. Closed Christmas. Domaine wines from Sancerre, Pouilly and Coteaux de Giennois. TF.WS.E.G.S. (☎ weekends.) www.gitton.fr E-mail: gittonvin@wanadoo.fr

FOR FURTHER INFORMATION
L'Union Viticole Sancerroise 9 rte de Chavignol, 18300 Sancerre. Tel: 02 48 78 51 03. Fax: 02 48 78 51 04.

known vineyard is the Chêne Marchand, which gives some of the finest wines. Another famous local vineyard is the Clos de la Poussie. At Bué, Le Caveau serves meals as well as the local wines.

A local cheese
The Monts Damnés vineyard is split between the two villages of Verdigny and Chavignol. This latter village has also given its name to the second local gastronomic specialty: the goat's milk cheese called Crottin de Chavignol, which is protected by its own *appellation contrôlée*. My French dictionary politely translates *crottin* as droppings – the cheese is, after all, small in size! It can be sampled, together with the local wine, in the underground Caves de la Mignonne, which are just north of Sancerre, on the road to Saint-Satur.

Pouilly-sur-Loire
If you take the D4 eastwards out of Sancerre, as soon as you have crossed the river Loire, you are in the vineyards of Pouilly. Here, two grapes are grown, the Sauvignon and the Chasselas.

Of these two, the Sauvignon makes the classic wine, the Pouilly Blanc Fumé, which is a similar wine to Sancerre though lacking some of its aggression. The Chasselas, on the other hand, is something of an historical anomaly. It was originally grown as a table grape for the Parisian market, but has remained to make an agreeable uncomplicated wine labeled as Pouilly-sur-Loire.

The largest producer of Pouilly Blanc Fumé is Patrick de Ladoucette, who owns the Château de Nozet, just north of the town of Pouilly. As well as making wine from his own

The Château de Nozet, where Patrick de Ladoucette makes much of the finest wine of Pouilly-Fumé.

vineyards, he buys both juice and wine from other growers. The finest wines from his own vines, he sells under a luxury presentation with the name of Baron de L.

Another attractive property producing full-bodied wines is the Château de Tracy, by the Loire just across from Sancerre.

Two hamlets whose names often appear on wine labels are les Loges and les Berthiers, on either side of the N7 trunk road, which now by-passes the town of Pouilly. At les Loges, the vineyards rise steeply above the Loire. Because it is a natural sun-trap, it produces perhaps the most full-bodied wines in the area.

Among the major vineyard owners of les Berthiers is the Domaine Saint-Michel, which also has vineyards in Burgundy, and which has behind it the Côte d'Or merchants Prosper Maufoux.

Prominent among the local growers are a number of members of the Dagueneau family.

POUILLY-SUR-LOIRE
Domaine Guy Saget
RN7, 58150 Pouilly-sur-Loire. Tel: 03 86 39 57 75. Fax: 03 86 39 08 30. (M. Jean-Louis Saget). Mon-Fri 0800-1200, 1400-1800. Sat, Sun by appointment only. Closed Christmas and New Year's Day. TF (with ☎ purchase of wine). WS.E. ☎
Masson-Blondelet 1 rue de Paris, 58150 Pouilly-sur-Loire. Tel: 03 86 39 00 34. Fax: 03 86 39 04 61. Open every day (except harvest), 0830-1200, 1330-1800. E.

WINE FESTIVAL
Pouilly-sur-Loire Second weekend in Aug.

FOR FURTHER INFORMATION
Syndicat Viticole de Pouilly les Loges, 58150 Pouilly-sur-Loire. Tel: 03 86 39 06 83. Fax: 03 86 39 06 88.

The Côte d'Or

DIJON
Cassis Boudier 14 rue de Cluj, 21007 Dijon. Tel: 03 80 74 33 33. Fax: 03 80 74 88 88. (M. Jean Battault). Mon-Fri 0900-1200, 1400-1730. Closed Aug. Working distillery making *crème de cassis* and other fruit liqueurs. TF. (charge for guided tour. TP for large groups) WS.E.G.S. ☎. E-mail: s.panijel@boudier.com

When one thinks of the wines of Burgundy, the first to come to mind are probably those of the Côte d'Or. While they only represent a small proportion of the total production, they include most of the great names.

No one knows for certain when the vines were first planted. There is evidence that the local inhabitants enjoyed wine as long ago as 500 B.C, for the difficult part of the tin road – from Cornwall to the eastern Mediterranean – lay between the headwaters of the river Seine and its tributaries and the valley of the river Saône. Here the Aedui, predecessors of the Burgundians, acted as porters – and they took wine as a significant part of their pay.

In about 400 B.C., a vast number of the Aedui crossed the Alps and settled in northern Italy. The main reason for this was, according to Plutarch, that "They found this drink so delicious that, on the spot, they prepared their arms and crossed the Alps, with their wives and children, in search of the country that produced such a wine."

It is probable that when they returned to Burgundy, a century and a half later, they brought vines and a knowledge of wine-making with them. It is certain that, during the Roman occupation, many wine estates were established in what are the better-known vineyard villages.

The wine of prince and prelate

With Burgundy's importance as an independent kingdom, and then as a semi-autonomous duchy, the reputation of its wines spread far and wide. Their fame, too, was helped by the fact that for more than six hundred years all the most famous vineyards belonged to either the nobility or the church. Thus the wines were drunk in all the most

Vines and poppies. Looking north to the hill of Corton (see page 48) from the direction of Beaune.

important royal and ecclesiastical circles in Europe.

Dijon

Dijon, the administrative and commercial capital of Burgundy, now has comparatively little to do with the wine trade. Industrial expansion has left little of the vineyards that it used to boast. However, it still has a high gastronomic reputation for its liqueurs, particularly the *crème de cassis de Dijon*, a controlled appellation, its gingerbread and its mustards. These and many other products are on show at the Dijon Gastronomic Fair, which takes place each year in early November.

The town center is still full of old streets, most of them just a short walk from the tourist office in the Place Darcy.

The cathedral of Saint-Bénigne is the fourth church on the site and dates from the end of the 13th century. Originally a Benedictine abbey, what used to be the monks' dormitory is now an archaeological museum.

Other churches that should be visited include Notre-Dame, Saint-Jean and Saint-Michel.

The former Palace of the Dukes of Burgundy now houses the Town Hall and what some people consider to be the best art gallery in France outside Paris.

To get to the Côte d'Or
From Chablis by the D91, A6 and A38, Dijon is 135 km (85 miles) and by the D91 and A6, Beaune is 130km (81 miles).

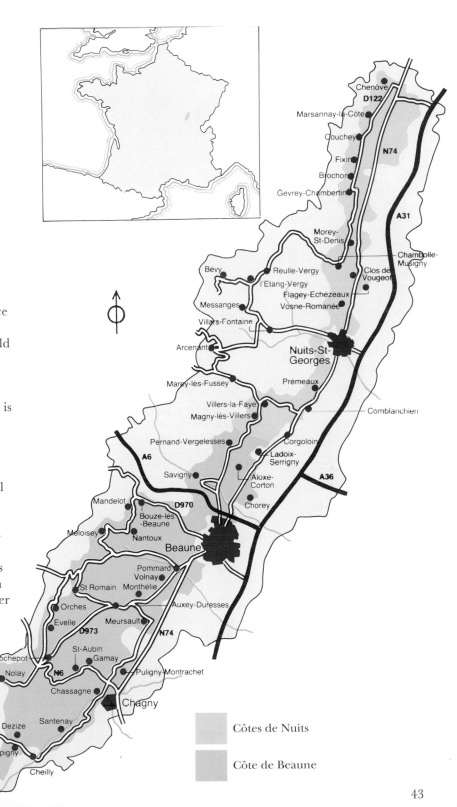

Côtes de Nuits

Côte de Beaune

The Côte de Nuits

GEVREY-CHAMBERTIN
Domaine du Clos de Tart Morey-Saint-Denis, 21220 Gevrey-Chambertin. Tel: 03 80 34 30 91. Fax: 03 80 24 60 01. (M. Pitiot). Mon-Fri 0900-1100, 1400-1700. Closed mid-Sep to mid-Oct. Two levels of cellars dug out of the rock. 16th-century wine-press. TP.WS.E. ☎

FIXIN
Domaine P. Gelin 2, rue du Chapitre, 21220 Fixin. Tel: 03 80 52 45 24. Fax: 03 80 51 47 80. Mon-Fri 0900-1200, 1400-1800. TF (with purchase). WS.

COUCHEY
Derey Frères 1 rue Jules-Ferry, Couchey, 21160 Marsannay-la-Côte. Tel: 03 80 52 15 04. Fax: 03 80 58 76 70. (M.Derey). Mon-Fri 0800-1200, 1400-1700. TF.WS.E.G.

MARSANNAY-LA-COTE
Domaine Fougeray de Beauclair 44, rue de Mazy, 21160 Marsannay-la-Côte. Tel: 03 80 52 21 12. Fax: 03 80 58 73 83. Mon-Sat 0800-1130, 1400-1730. Sun 1000-1200. TF.WS.E. ☎ E-mail: fougeraydebeauclair@ wanadoo.fr www.caves-particulieres.com/ membres/fougeray

VOUGEOT
Château de la Tour Clos de Vougeot, 21640 Vougeot. Tel: 03 80 62 86 13. Fax: 03 80 62 82 72. (M. or Mme Labet). Every day except Mon 1000-1900. Closed end Nov-1 Apr. Typical vaulted cellars within Clos de Vougeot itself. Largest owners of vines in Clos de Vougeot. TF (with purchase). WS.E. E-mail: labet@axnet.fr

A choice of routes

Driving south from Dijon along the Côte d'Or, the motorist has a choice of three roads. If you are in a hurry, take the A31 motorway and then, to visit the vineyards, take the exit either at Nuits-Saint-Georges or at Beaune. Alternatively, take the N74 màin road, which has lesser vineyards on either side, or D122, the *Route des Grands Crus*, which slowly wanders through the famous wine villages of Burgundy.

Chenôve

To join the *Route des Grands Crus*, take the N74 and after some 5km (3 miles), at Chenôve, turn right at the L'Escargotière restaurant.

The vineyards of Chenôve have suffered greatly from the expansion of the city of Dijon and there are now only a quarter of the growers that there were 25 years ago. The most important feature in the village is the former press-house of the Dukes of Burgundy, with two enormous wine-presses dating back to 1238.

The first vineyard village of importance is Marsannay-la-Côte, which has traditionally been known for the best rosé wines in Burgundy. It has recently been granted its own village *appellation* for white and red wines, so there is a real danger that the rosé wines may slowly disappear. The next village, Couchey, also has the right to sell its wines under the name of Marsannay.

Fixin may be said to be the first village on the Côte to produce great red wines, with the Clos de la Perrière probably being the outstanding vineyard.

A souvenir of Napoleon

For Imperialists, the village is a living memory to the Emperor Napoleon, thanks to an adopted son of the village, Claude Noisot. He shared Napoleon's exile at Elba and fought at the battle of Waterloo. In later life, Napoleon became his fixation. He renamed a local vineyard Clos Napoleon and created a park in his memory, with, eventually, a museum, a florid statue of the Emperor rising to lead the world again, and his own tomb, where he was buried, standing on guard.

Gevrey-Chambertin

After Brochon comes Gevrey-Chambertin, perhaps the capital of the red wines of Burgundy. Driving along on the southern side of the village, the vineyards read like a roll-call of honor: Mazis-Chambertin, Ruchottes-Chambertin, Clos de Bèze, le Chambertin and Latricières-Chambertin.

On looking at the soil there is little to show that where the sign reads *Ici commence le Chambertin*, real greatness begins.

Morey

Like many of the villages of Burgundy, Morey has tacked on to its name that of its most famous vineyard, the Clos Saint Denis, and has become Morey-Saint-Denis. Its other greatest vineyards are the Clos de la Roche, the Clos de Tart and the Clos des Lambrays.

Chambolle-Musigny

The vineyard of Bonnes-Mares is shared by Morey with its neighbor Chambolle-Musigny. Here the finest wines come from le Musigny, which makes a minute quantity of white wine each year, in addition to an outstanding red. In the center of the village is a magnificent lime tree planted on the instructions of Sully, Henri IV's minister.

Clos de Vougeot

Down the slope from the vineyard of le Musigny is the Clos de Vougeot, a walled vineyard founded in the 12th century by the monks of Cîteaux. Within the *clos* of 50 hectares (120 acres), there are almost 80 owners, each making his own wine. The Château, which now belongs to the *Confrérie des Chevaliers du Tastevin*, was originally built as the press-house and cellars for the monks.

WINE MUSEUM
Château du Vougeot
21640 Vougeot. Tel: 03 80 62 86 09. Fax: 03 80 62 82 75. Mon-Fri 0900-1830, Sat 0900-1700. Collection of old wine implements. Press-house, with four old presses. G.
www.closdevougeot.com

WINE FESTIVAL
Morey-St.-Denis
Carrefour de Dionysos, 1st. Fri in Apr.

The Clos de Vougeot, the largest vineyard in the Côte d'Or. The château was once the center of the wine domaine of the Cistercian order of monks. Now it is the headquarters of the local drinking brotherhood, the Confrérie des Chevaliers du Tastevin. *Famous for their extremely sociable lifestyle, they award their label to outstanding wines from Burgundy. An example is on page 34.*

NUITS-ST.-GEORGES
Domaine de Loisy 28, rue Général de Gaulle, 21700 Nuits-St.-Georges. Tel: 03 80 61 02 72. Fax: 03 80 61 36 14. (Mme Françoise de Loisy Loquin). Bed and breakfast. WS.E.I. ☎

Moillard-Grivot 74, rte Nationale, 21700 Nuits-St.-Georges. Tel: 03 80 62 42 20. Fax: 03 80 61 28 13. Mon-Sun 1000-1800. Closed Jan. Cellar visit. TF. (TP for groups) WS.E. E-mail: nulcave@wanadoo.fr

Morin Père et Fils 9, quai Fleury, 21700 Nuits-St.-Georges. Tel: 03 80 61 19 51. Fax: 03 80 61 05 10. Every day. 15 Mar-31 Oct 0900-1900. Rest of year 0900-1200, 1400-1800. 18th-century cellars, guided tours, old vintage wines. TF. (TP ☎ for groups) WS.G.

VOSNE-ROMANEE
Domaine Lamarche 9, rue des Communes, 21700 Vosne-Romanée. Tel: 03 80 61 07 94. Fax: 03 80 61 24 31. (M. or Mme Lamarche). Mon-Fri 0900-1200, 1400-1700. Closed 2nd half of Aug and 1st. week in Sep. TF (with purchase) E. www.domaine.lamarche.com

Domaine Armelle et Bernard Rion 8, rte Nationale, 21700 Vosne-Romanée. Tel: 03 80 61 05 31. Fax: 03 80 61 34 60. (M. Bernard Rion). Mon-Sat 0900-1900. By appointment only. M. Rion also breeds Bearded Collies and Berger de Brie dogs, and is happy to show them to visitors. TF (with purchase). WS.E. ☎ www.webiwine.com/rion

WINE FESTIVALS
Nuits-St.-Georges Sale of wines from the Hospices de Nuits, 1st. Sun in Apr.

Vougeot's second castle, the Château de la Tour, was built at the end of the 19th century. The "new" château has beneath it some magnificent cellars dating back to the 15th century. Unfortunately it is not open to the public.

In the narrow streets there is a particularly fine collection of vineyard owners' houses. One in the Rue Ste. Barbe has a wooden balustrade more than 400 years old.

After Vougeot, the next vineyards belong to the village of Flagey-Echezeaux. As the village lies to the east of the main road and is undistinguished, its claim to fame must be its two *grands crus*: les Echezeaux and les Grands Echezeaux. Its lesser wines can be sold under the name of the next, and infinitely more famous, village of Vosne-Romanée.

Harvest time in some of the most expensive agricultural land in the world, the vineyard of Romanée-Conti. In the early 1900s, many Burgundian villages added their name to that of the most famous vineyard. Thus Vosne became Vosne-Romanée.

Vosne-Romanée
In the crown of the red wines of Burgundy, this must be the diamond in the center. Its wines have gained a justified reputation for their unrivalled finesse and bouquet.

While some would claim that the Romanée-Conti is the finest, there are others who would vote for La Tâche. Close behind come such other great wines as La Romanée, Romanée-Saint-Vivant, Richebourg and La Grande Rue.

Romanée-Conti and La Tâche belong exclusively to the Domaine de la Romanée-Conti, La Romanée to the Liger-Belair family, and La Grande Rue to the Lamarche domain. Given these circumstances, each bottle is allocated carefully – and at a price.

Once again, there is little to distinguish these noble plots of earth. To visit them, you go up the narrow lane by the side of the church. On the slope in front of you, a simple cross marks Romanée-Conti.

Nuits-Saint-Georges

Because the main road skirts the fringes of Nuits-Saint-Georges, few visit the town itself. Besides its host of merchants' cellars (Nuits comes second only to Beaune in importance in the Burgundy wine trade) there is the beautiful 13th-century church of St. Symphorien.

Though it has been much destroyed in a succession of wars, the town still maintains a bustling air of history. The fame of its wines owes a great deal to the prescriptions of the royal physician Fagon, who cured Louis XIV of a fistula by liberally dosing him with Nuits. In honor of this, the main street is now named after him.

The importance of the town and its wines have led to this northern part of the Côte d'Or vineyards being called the Côte de Nuits.

Prémeaux

South of Nuits, the next village is Prémeaux, within whose boundaries are produced many of the finest *premier cru* wines of Nuits-Saint-Georges.

Prémeaux also has a number of natural springs, and until 1970 the water from one of them was marketed commercially. Its medical properties were recognized in Roman times.

Comblanchien and Corgoloin

The Côte de Nuits finishes with the two villages of Comblanchien and Corgoloin. Sadly, neither has been able to establish an individual reputation for its wines and they are sold simply as Côte de Nuits Villages.

Comblanchien is perhaps better known now for its "marble" (actually a variety of limestone that looks like marble), which was widely used in the construction of the Paris Opéra and Orly airport.

The domaine *of the vineyard of Clos de Tart at Morey-Saint-Denis takes its name from its medieval owners, the nuns of Tart-le-Bas.*

The name of the last vineyard on the Côte de Nuits, the Clos de Langres, is an indication of the former importance of the Church in the history of viticulture. It used to be the property of the Bishop and Chapter of Langres, a town to the north of Dijon, who, until the Revolution, were the largest vineyard owners in Burgundy, after the Cistercian order of monks.

CORGOLOIN
Domaine d'Ardhuy
Clos des Langres, 21700 Corgoloin. Tel: 03 80 62 98 73. Fax: 03 80 62 95 15. (Blandine d'Ardhuy). Mon-Sat 0900-1230, 1400-1800. Sun by appointment. Closed Christmas to New Year's Day. 18th-century wine-press. Collection of old wine-making implements. Historic vaulted cellars. TF.WS.E.S.

Red Wines of the Côte de Beaune

The *Route des Grands Crus* on the Côte de Nuits is relatively easy to follow, for the villages form a straight line. On the Côte de Beaune, by way of contrast, there are numerous twists and turns and often there can be a choice of roads.

Corton and Corton-Charlemagne

Ladoix-Serrigny is the first of the villages that one comes to; the reputation of wines under its own name comes below those that it makes on its higher slopes, which can be sold under the *grand cru* names of Corton Charlemagne for white wines and, with rare exceptions, Corton for red. (One exception is the Cuvée Paul Chanson belonging to the Hospices de Beaune, which is a white wine coming from Corton-Vergennes.)

The village of Aloxe-Corton, with the intricately-decorated roof of Château Corton-André in the center. Its two neighboring villages can also use its name for their wines.

To the left of the main road, as you come out of the village there is an 11th-century chapel, probably built for pilgrims on their way to Santiago de Compostella.

Aloxe-Corton

Aloxe-Corton, as well as its *grand cru* vineyards, boasts the colorfully roofed Château Corton-André built at the end of the last century and the more sober Château Corton-Grancey, belonging to wine company Louis Latour. Behind it, carved out of a quarry, are perhaps the finest cellars in Burgundy, with the estate press-house above.

The third of the villages producing Corton and Corton-Charlemagne is Pernand-Vergelesses. Tucked into a narrow valley in the hillside, it is perhaps the least spoilt of all the wine villages of the Côte d'Or, with some beautiful growers' houses.

Savigny and Chorey-lès-Beaune

Savigny is particularly known for its red wines. In the valley lies an imposing château, which was rebuilt at the beginning of the 18th century, and which now houses a car museum. Leading up from the village is the valley of the Fontaine Froide, a beautiful drive for those tired of looking at vineyards. At the top of the valley lies the pretty village of Bouilland, with its excellent restaurant, the Vieux Moulin.

On the plain, beyond the N74, is the village of Chorey-lès-Beaune, where a number of important estates are based. The church has a belfry in the "foreign" style of Franche-Comté and there is a picturesque château surrounded by a moat.

*Vintage time in Burgundy.
Emptying the plastic crates of
freshly-picked grapes into the
trailer for them to be taken back
into the press-house.*

**CHOREY-LES-BEAUNE
Domaine Germain**
Château de Chorey-lès-
Beaune, 21200 Beaune.
Tel: 03 80 22 06 05. Fax:
03 80 24 03 93. (François
or Estelle Germain). Mon-
Sat 0900-1200, 1400-1800.
Attractive château, rebuilt
in 1668. Bed and breakfast.
TF.WS.E.G.
E-mail: domaine.germain@
wanadoo.fr

**PERNAND-
VERGELESSES
Domaine P. Dubreuil-
Fontaine Père et Fils**
21420 Pernand-Vergelesses.
Tel: 03 80 21 55 43.
Fax: 03 80 21 51 69.
Mon-Fri 0900-1200,
1400-1800; Sat 0900-1200.
Closed Sun, holidays,
1-25 Aug. TF.WS.E.G. ☎

**POMMARD
Château de Pommard**
21630 Pommard. Tel: 03
80 22 07 99. Fax: 03 80 24
65 88. Every day 0900-
1800. Closed 3rd Sun in
Nov-31 Mar. Beautiful
cellars and buildings.
TP.WS.E.G. ☎

Pommard

The first vineyard village after
Beaune is Pommard, famous
throughout the world for its full-
bodied red wines. The main street
winds off to the right from the
D973, with growers' houses on
both sides.

The village has three châteaux,
two of which have now been
united as the Château de
Pommard and belong to the
Laplanche family. The oldest is the
Château de la Commaraine
belonging to the Jaboulet-
Vercherre family and backing on
to the attractive Clos de la
Commaraine vineyard.

Volnay

As another village standing back
from and above the main road,
Volnay maintains an agreeable
calm, with its finest vineyards lying
out on the slope in front of it.

In historical times, the Dukes of
Burgundy spent the summers in the
château that they built here,
though unfortunately its
destruction was ordered by
Cardinal Richelieu.

Traditionally, each May Day a
shooting competition was held
within the village, with the winner
being able to style himself as
"King" and gain exemption from
certain taxes.

Monthélie

To find the village of Monthélie,
you must turn right off the main
road on to the D23. It is a village
of narrow streets and wine
growers' houses spread down the
hillside and with a reputation of
poverty, because there are no
sources of water on its territory. As
Monthélie is slightly off the main
road, its wines have not the quality
image that they so rightly deserve.

The Town of Beaune

BEAUNE
Caves Exposition Reine Pédauque Porte Saint Nicolas, 21200 Beaune. Tel: 03 80 22 23 11. Fax: 03 80 22 70 20. Every day 0900-1130, 1400-1730 (Jun-Sep 1400-1800), closed first 3 weeks Jan. Groups by appointment. T.P.W.S.E.
Domaine Albert Morot Château de la Creusotte, 21200 Beaune. Tel: 03 80 22 35 39. Fax: 03 80 22 47 50. Every day 1000-1200, 1400-1800. Guided tour of cellars and press-house with talk on wine-making. T.P.W.S.E.
Albert Ponnelle Clos St-Nicolas 38 Faubourg St.-Nicolas, 21200 Beaune. Tel: 03 80 22 00 05. Fax: 03 80 24 19 73. Every day in May-Sep, 0930-1900, Oct-Apr, Mon-Fri, 0800-1200, 1400-1800. 14th-century cellars. T.E.W.S.E.G. ☎ E-mail: albert.ponnelle@wanadoo.fr
Hôtel-Dieu Tel: 03 80 24 45 00. Fax: 03 80 24 45 99. Apr-Oct 0900-1830, Nov-Mar 0900-1130, 1400-1730. G. E-mail: hospices-beaune@ wanadoo.fr. www.hospices-de-beaune.tm.fr
Musée du Vin de Bourgogne rue d'Enfer, 21200 Beaune. Tel: 03 80 24 56 92. Fax: 03 80 24 56 20. Located in former palace of Dukes of Burgundy. Every day 0930-1800 (closed Tue from Dec to Mar). I.N.

WINE FESTIVALS
Beaune *Foire de Beaune* end May-1st. week of Jun. *Les Trois Glorieuses* weekend of 3rd Sun in Nov. Auction of Hospices wines on the Sun.

FOR FURTHER INFORMATION
B.I.V.B. 12, bvd Bretonnière, 21200 Beaune. Tel: 03 80 25 04 80. Fax: 03 80 25 04 81. www.bivb.com

Beaune must be one of the most satisfying wine towns to visit because of its compactness. It is still circled by its town walls, built in the 13th and 14th centuries, and, while the town has now expanded far beyond this military corset, most that is of interest lies within. The origins of the town go back to Roman days and on a town plan the circular trace of the *oppidum* can still be seen.

In these days of peace, the walls and towers of the fortifications are used to store wine, and while expanding business and modern machinery have led many companies to construct new premises outside the town, most of the important ones still have their offices and much of their stock in the town center.

While Bouchard Père et Fils and Chanson Père et Fils store their wine in the bastions with walls up to seven meters (22 ft) thick, other companies, such as Patriarche and Ponnelle, use dispossessed religious properties. Drouhin have the former cellars of the Dukes of Burgundy.

The Hôtel-Dieu

Among the architectural gems of the town, the most famous must be the Hôtel-Dieu, built in 1443 by Nicolas Rolin, Chancellor of the Duchy of Burgundy, as a "hospital for the accommodation and assistance of the poor and the sick." Built in the Flemish style, with high, colorful roofs, around a beautiful courtyard, its treasures include a polyptych of the Last Judgment by Roger van der Weyden.

The Hôtel-Dieu forms part of the Hospices de Beaune (the other part is the Hospice de la Charité in the rue de Lorraine) financed by considerable endowments, including an important

estate of vineyards, whose wine is auctioned off each year on the third Sunday in November.

In the picturesquely named rue d'Enfer is the former Palace of the Dukes of Burgundy, which now houses an attractively laid out wine museum. Close to this is Notre-Dame, the parish church of Beaune.

Other buildings of interest include the Town Hall in what used to be the cloister of an Ursuline

convent and, beyond the town wall on the road to the north, the simple 13th-century church of St. Nicolas.

To the west of the town, on the flanks of the hillsides split by two valleys, lie the vineyards that have made Beaune so rich and spread its name throughout the world. While nearly all the wine that is made is red, the variety of soils and microclimates give a variety of styles that is matched by the wines of no other commune in Burgundy. There are devotees of the Grèves vineyard, of the Clos des Mouches, of Bressandes and of Fèves; each gives a great wine in its individual style.

Until comparatively recently, there was been a grave shortage of reasonably priced hotel rooms in Beaune. This problem has now been solved and today it is a good halt on the motorway for a one-night stay, or longer.

The courtyard of the Hôtel-Dieu at Beaune. This building dates back to the beginning of the 15th century, when the Duchy of Burgundy stretched as far as the Low Countries, which accounts for the architecture, most particularly of the roofs, which are tiled in the Flemish style.

Built as a hospital for old people, it is financed by large endowments, particularly vineyards, that have been made over the centuries.

White Wines of the Côte de Beaune

AUXEY-DURESSES
Domaine Roy Auxey-Duresses, 21190 Meursault. Tel: 03 80 21 22 37. Fax: 03 80 21 23 71. (M. Roy). Every day 0900-1900. TF.WS.

MEURSAULT
Château de Meursault 21190 Meursault. Tel: 03 80 26 22 75. Fax: 03 80 26 22 76. Every day 0930-1200, 1430-1800. Closed Dec-Jan. Art gallery, 14th-century cellars. TP.WS.E.
Le Manoir Murisaltien 4, rue du Clos de Mazeray, 21190 Meursault. Tel: 03 80 21 21 83. Fax: 03 80 21 66 48. (M. Marc Dumont). Mon-Fri 0800-1200, 1400-1800. Closed first 3 weeks Aug. (Also own Château Demessey, see page 58.) TF. (TP ☎ for groups). WS.E.
Domaine Jacques Prieur 6 rue des Santenots, 21190 Meursault. Tel: 03 80 21 23 85. Fax: 03 80 21 29 19. Mon-Fri. Closed Aug. WS.E. ☎
Ropiteau Frères 13, rue du 11 Novembre, 21190 Meursault. Tel/Fax: 03 80 21 24 73. (Monica van der Stap). Every day 0900-1900. Closed 21 Nov-Easter. 15th-century cellars, formerly the property of the Hospices de Beaune. TF (depending on wine). WS.E.G.N.S. (☎ for groups.)

Traditionally, grapes in Burgundy have always been picked by hand, but difficulty in obtaining the necessary labor exactly when it is needed is leading some growers, such as this one in Meursault, to turn to mechanical harvesters.

While there are some who might claim that Burgundy does not produce the finest red wines of France, there are few who would say that it does not make the best dry white wines. Here come together the perfect blend of soil, climate and the Chardonnay grape to give great wines with fruit and flavor.

The village of Aloxe-Corton produces great white wines in the Charlemagne vineyard, but it is the three villages of Meursault, Puligny-Montrachet and Chassagne-Montrachet that bear the reputation for making the best of the white wines.

Meursault
Meursault is a useful center for visiting the vineyards of the Côte d'Or. There are a number of small hotels and restaurants and a camping site, with a swimming-pool.

The village has two châteaux. The older, dating from the 14th century, was largely destroyed in 1478; what remains now forms part of the town hall. The Château de Meursault is built above the 14th-century cellars of the Cistercian monks. Here there is now an art gallery and the chance to taste a range of fine burgundies.

On the main N74 road are the ruins of a leper-house, built in 1180 by Hugues de Bourgogne. The village church is also worth visiting. Its most outstanding feature is its spire, the tallest in the region.

Puligny-Montrachet
Puligny-Montrachet is a much quieter village, with its two squares ringed by imposing private houses. Once again there are two châteaux. The "old" one was partly dismantled and sold off to antique dealers during World War I. The "Château de Puligny-Montrachet" dates back to the middle of the 18th century. Its main claim to fame, apart from its wines, appears to be the fact that Laetizia Ramolino, Napoleon's mother, once slept there.

The great vineyards lie behind the village. Two *grands crus,* Chevalier-Montrachet and Bienvenues-Bâtard-Montrachet, lie solely within the boundaries; two others, le Montrachet and Bâtard-Montrachet, it shares with its neighbor, Chassagne.

Le Montrachet

Le Montrachet is considered by many to be the world's greatest dry white wine. The vineyard that produces it is just under 8 hectares (20 acres) in size, and has 15 different owners, with their own parcels of vines. In an average year, one of these may produce no more than a single barrel – yet each bottle may sell at £100 ($150) or even more.

Chassagne-Montrachet is best known for its white wines, but it actually produces rather more red wine, much of it of a very high quality. The village I find to be something of a disappointment.

Santenay

From Chassagne, the vineyard road, the D113A, curves round the hillside to the last of the major vineyard villages, Santenay. Here, mainly red wines are made.

Santenay has medicinal springs. The water is useful in the treatment of such potential local problems as liver malfunctions, diabetes, obesity and gout. Perhaps more importantly, they entitle Santenay to a casino!

So far, we have kept along the straight road through the vineyards. However, there are villages lying off that road in the valleys to the west.

From Meursault, the D17E leads first to Auxey-Duresses, known for its red and white wines. Next comes the

Through the bars of a gateway in the surrounding wall can be seen the vines of the vineyard of le Montrachet, thought by many to produce the finest white wine in the world.

attractive village of Saint-Romain, split into two parts, one on a rocky escarpment, the other in the valley below. There are the remains of a château that dates back to at least the 10th century and which used to belong to the Dukes of Burgundy.

Caves in the imposing cliffs that overlook the village sheltered prehistoric man and there is a small museum of local history in the town hall. Also of interest is a cooperage whose casks might just as well be found in California as Burgundy. The N6, which was the main road from Paris to the south until the motorway was built, leads up to the village of Gamay, which gave its name to the grape, and Saint-Aubin, which produces excellent red and white wines. It is in villages like these that real bargains are to be found.

MONTHELIE
Domaine Michel Dupont-Fahn Clos des Toisières, 21190 Monthélie. Tel: 03 80 21 26 78. Fax: 03 80 21 21 22. (Michel or Leslie Dupont-Fahn). Mon-Fri 0900-1200, 1400-1700. Closed Aug. By appointment only. TF.E. ☎

CHASSAGNE-MONTRACHET
Domaine Jean Pillot et fils RN6, 21190 Chassagne-Montrachet. Tel: 03 80 21 92 96. Fax: 03 80 21 92 57. (Jean-Marc Pillot). Mon-Fri 0900-1200, 1400-1700. By appointment only. TF.G. ☎

PULIGNY-MONTRACHET
Domaine Chartron 13, Grande Rue, 21190 Puligny-Montrachet. Tel: 03 80 21 32 85. Fax: 03 80 21 36 35. Every day 1000-1200, 1400-1800. Open 1 Apr-31 Nov. TF (TP for groups). WS.E.G. ☎ E-mail: info@chartron-trebuchet.com www.chartron-trebuchet.com

ST.-AUBIN
Hubert Lamy St.-Aubin, 21190 Meursault. Tel: 03 80 21 32 55. Fax: 03 80 21 38 32. (Mme. Lamy). Mon-Sat. TP.WS. ☎

WINE FESTIVALS
Meursault
La Trinquée de Meursault, second Sat in Sep.

La Paulée de Meursault, Mon of third weekend in Nov.

The Hautes-Côtes

HAUTES-COTES DE BEAUNE
Domaine Mazilly Père et Fils Meloisey, 21190 Meursault. Tel: 03 80 26 02 00. Fax: 03 80 26 03 67. Every day 0900-1900. By appointment. TF (with purchase). WS.E. ☎
J. Joliot et Fils Nantoux, 21190 Meursault. Tel: 03 80 26 01 44. Fax: 03 80 26 03 55. (M. J.B. Joliot). Every day 0800-2000. Picnic area. TF.WS. ☎ www.avco.org/joliot
HAUTES-COTES DE NUITS
Domaine de Montmain Villars-Fontaine, 21700 Nuits-St.-Georges. Tel: 03 80 62 31 94. Fax: 03 80 61 02 31. (Bernard Hudelot). TF.WS.G. ☎ www.perso.wanadoo. fr/bernard.hudelot/index.htm
Domaine Thévenot-le-Brun et Fils Marey-lès-Fussey, 21700 Nuits-St.-Georges. Tel: 03 80 62 91 64. Fax: 03 80 62 99 81. Mon-Sat 0800-1200, 1400-1800. TF.WS.E. (☎ Sat, groups). E-mail: thevenot-le-brun@ wanadoo.fr

Behind the main vineyards of the Côte d'Or lie others in what is known as the Hautes-Côtes. Here there are not just vines, but also meadows and plantings of soft fruit, particularly blackcurrants, for the *crème de cassis* liqueur.

Most of the wine that is made is red, though there is also a little white, and much of it is made at the co-operative cellar of the Hautes-Côtes, which is on the N74, on the southern outskirts of Beaune.

The scenery is spectacular. From the top of the cliff at Orches you look down on Saint-Romain, the valley leading down to Meursault, the plain of the Saône, the Jura mountains and, on a very clear day, Mont Blanc.

There is the Château de la Rochepot, nestling in against the hillside; the Pas Saint Martin, near Mandelot, where the saint is reputed to have escaped from the Devil by jumping across the valley; the pretty town of Nolay, with its 14th-century market hall; and Bévy, with the biggest vineyard area of all, where a

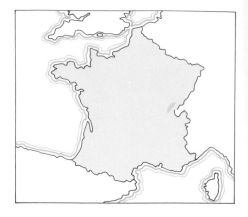

local wine-merchant reclaimed land that had been scrub for generations.

This is the quieter, less commercial face of Burgundy, where time seems less important. Many of the growers also own vines in the more fancied villages of the Côte – but their prices always seem more reasonable, because they do not have a fashionable address.

To taste a range of the wines, and simple local food, there is no better place to go than the Maison des Hautes-Côtes, a joint venture of a number of growers at Marey-lès-Fussey on the D8, in the hills above Corgoloin.

At Orches, above Pommard, there are two specialties, a rosé wine and Poire Williams distilled from fruit from the local orchards.

The Hautes-Côtes are visited by too few. They can be seen in half a day – but it is worthwhile taking longer. While the local description of them as the "Switzerland of Burgundy" seems something of an exaggeration, their quietness, and the variegated landscape, make a relaxing change.

The Château de la Rochepot was built in the 15th century by Regnier Pot. Almost totally destroyed during the Revolution, it was restored by the French President Sadi Carnot.

The Jura

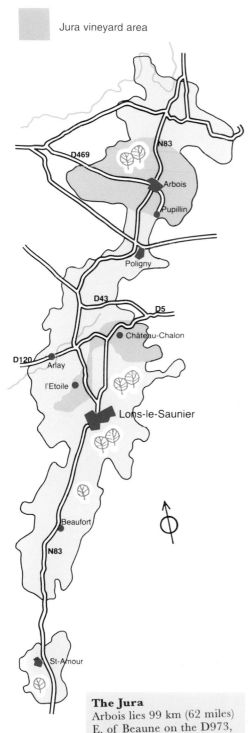

Jura vineyard area

The Jura
Arbois lies 99 km (62 miles)
E. of Beaune on the D973,
N73, N5 and D469.

For what is a comparatively small vineyard area, the Jura produces a remarkably diverse selection of wines. The capital of the region is Arbois, a charming town whose architecture has been influenced by long-past Spanish occupation. It is particularly well known for its rosé wines, reputedly the best in France after Tavel.

More individual is the *vin jaune*, which tastes like a fino sherry and is produced in a similar way. The best of this comes from the small village of Château-Châlon. It is bottled in a traditional bottle called a *clavelin*, containing just 62cl of wine.

Other local specialties are the rich *vin de paille* and the aperitif *macvin*, made like port.

The wines of the Jura are too often forgotten. In some ways they are among the most traditional in France, made in ways and from grapes that are not used elsewhere. The vineyards are worth a visit in their own right, either on the way to Geneva and the ski-resorts, or as a day off from the bustle of Burgundy.

ARBOIS
Fruitière Vinicole d'Arbois
2, rue des Fossés, 39600
Arbois. Tel: 03 84 66 11 67.
Fax: 03 84 37 48 80. Summer,
every day 0900-2000. Rest
of year by appointment.
Founded 1906. T.P.WS.E.G.
Henri Maire S.A.
Domaine de Boichailles,
39600 Arbois. Tel: 03 84 66
15 27. Fax: 03 84 66 42 42.
(Isabelle Ravix.) Every day
0900-1900. Audio-visual
presentation, wine tasting,
vineyard visit. T.F.WS.E.G.
www.henri-maire.com
ARLAY
Château d'Arlay 39140
Arlay. Tel: 03 84 85 04 22.
Fax: 03 84 48 17 96. Mon-
Sat 0900-1200, 1400-1800,
Sunday by appointment.
Château visits every
afternoon in Jul and Aug.
Gardens, park and aviary
open to visitors, afternoons
15 Jun-15 Sep. T.F.WS.E.S.
www.caves-particulieres.com/
membres/arlay
FOR FURTHER INFORMATION
C.I.V.J. B.P. 41, 39602
Arbois. Tel: 03 84 66 26 14.
G. www.jura-vins.com

Henri Maire's tasting-cellar.
There are no charges for visits.

The Côte Chalonnaise

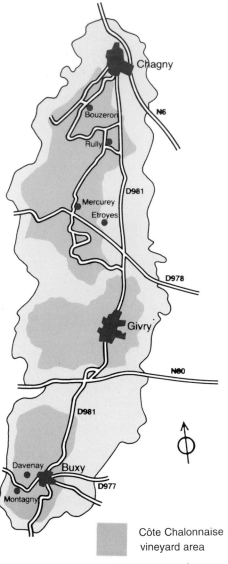

Côte Chalonnaise
vineyard area

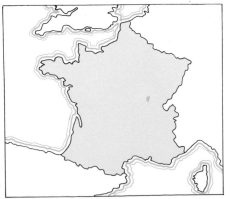

For too long the wines of the Côte Chalonnaise have been under-appreciated, but recently there have been two moves to give them more of an individual personality. First, the Aligoté wines from the small village of Bouzeron have been able to call themselves *appellation* Bouzeron – and no other village in Burgundy has been permitted to use its name in this way.

Secondly, up just one level, the red and white wines have been able to add Côte Chalonnaise to their generic name of Bourgogne. This is important, for the wines from the local vineyards, apart from those from the four village *appellations* of Rully, Mercurey, Givry and Montagny, had too often disappeared anonymously into the blending vats of the large merchants.

Chagny

The starting point for a visit to the vineyards of the Côte Chalonnaise must be the town of Chagny. From there, you take the D981 road to the south, though diversions must regularly be taken to the right to visit the various villages.

Bouzeron

Of these the first is Bouzeron, already mentioned for its Aligotés. The monks of Cluny were the first to establish the reputation of Bouzeron's wines, but now Bouchard Père et Fils and Aubert de Villaine, one of the co-owners of the Domaine de la Romanée-Conti, have important holdings here.

Rully

There is a rather steep and narrow road to the next village, Rully, but the faint-hearted may prefer to

MONTAGNY
Le Cellier Buxynois
rte de Cluny, 71390 Buxy.
Tel: 03 85 92 04 14.
Fax: 03 85 92 10 89. Mon-Sat 0830-1200, 1400-1800.
TF (with purchase).WS.

BOUZERON
Chanzy Frères
Domaine de l'Hermitage, Bouzeron, 71150 Chagny.
Tel: 03 85 87 23 69. Fax: 03 85 91 24 92. (Daniel Chanzy). Mon-Fri 0830-1200, 1400-1800. Sat by appointment. Closed 1st. fortnight Aug. TF.WS. ☎ E-mail: daniel.chanzy@ wanadoo.fr www.chanzy.com

RULLY
André Delorme rue de la République, 71150 Rully.
Tel: 03 85 87 10 12. Fax: 03 85 87 04 60. Mon-Sat 0830-1200, 1330-1700. Still and sparkling wines from Côte Chalonnaise. TF.WS.E.

Jérôme Noël-Bouton Domaine de la Folie, 71150 Chagny. Tel: 03 85 87 18 59. Fax: 03 85 87 03 53. (Jérôme Noël-Bouton). Every day 0900-1830. TF.WS.E.

MERCUREY
Antonin Rodet 71640 Mercurey. Tel: 03 85 98 12 12. Fax: 03 85 45 25 49. Mon-Thu 0800-1200, 1400-1800. Fri 0800-1200, 1400-1700. Tasting in cellars. TF.WS.E. (G by appointment) www.rodet.com

WINE FESTIVALS
Concours des Vins de la Côte Chalonnaise et du Couchois Second Sat in Jan (location varies).

Chagny Wine Fair, about 15 Aug, 4-5 days.

return to Chagny first. Rully has suffered badly in history and its reputation for its wines has improved largely as a result of the efforts of its dynamic mayor, Jean-François Delorme. As well as making fine red and white wines, it is also a center of the sparkling-wine trade.

Mercurey

The best-known wines of the Côte are Mercurey, and they come from a cluster of small villages of which Mercurey is one. It is known especially for its red wines, which have an equal standing to many from the Côte d'Or.

There are certain "château" wines with a good reputation. The one most often found is the Château de Chamirey, from local merchants Antonin Rodet.

Givry and Montagny

Givry, too, is well-known for its red wines, though it produces much less than Mercurey. It was a favorite of Henri IV (who always seemed to be prepared to endorse the local wine) and he may well have used it as an aid in his courtship of his local girlfriend, Gabrielle d'Estrées.

The last of the wines of the Côte Chalonnaise is Montagny. This is just white wine from the vineyards around the small town of Buxy, where there is a tasting cellar in the Tour Rouge.

The Château de Chamirey at Mercurey, which belongs to the Marquis de Jouennes, Chairman of local wine company Antonin Rodet. The château vineyard produces both red and white wine with the appellation *Mercurey.*

The Mâconnais

CLESSE
Jean Thévenet
Quintaine-Clessé, 71260 Clessé. Tel: 03 85 36 94 03. Fax: 03 85 36 99 25. Mon-Fri. TF.WS.E. ☎

IGE
Groupement de Producteurs les Vignerons d'Igé 71960 Igé. Tel: 03 85 33 33 56. Fax: 03 85 33 41 85. Mon-Sat 0800-1200, 1400-1800. TF.WS.E.

Caveau de Domange
11th-century church, collection of old wine implements. Open Sun, holidays 1000-1200, 1400-1900. Closed Dec-Mar.

LUGNY
Caveau St.-Pierre 71260 Lugny. Tel/Fax: 03 85 33 20 27. Mon 0900-1500, Tue-Sun 0900-2100. Closed Mon. Restaurant. TP.WS.E. ☎

OZENAY
Château Demessey
71700 Ozenay. Tel: 03 85 32 57 30. Fax: 03 85 51 33 82. (M. and Mme. Fachon). Every day 0900-2000. Closed Jan. Historic buildings, accommodations available in 15th-century vineyard workers' cottages. TF (TP for groups). WS.E. ☎

VIRE
Domaine André Bonhomme 71260 Viré. Tel: 03 85 33 11 86. Fax: 03 85 33 93 51. Every day 0800-2000. Underground cellar. TF.WS.E. ☎

Cave de Viré La Passion Partagée, Cave de Viré, En Vercheron, 71260 Viré. Tel: 03 85 32 25 50. Fax: 03 85 32 25 55. Mon-Fri 0800-1200, 1400-1800 (Fri 1700). Tasting cellar open Sat, Sun. TF.WS.E.S. E-mail: cavedevire@wanadoo.fr www.winecollection.com/vin/proprio/fr/p48.htm

All that now remains of the Benedictine Abbey of Cluny, once the most important church building in Europe after St. Peter's in Rome.

If you continue along the D981 road that has taken you through the vineyards of the Côte Chalonnaise you cross the boundary into the vineyards of the Mâconnais at the village of Saint-Gengoux-le-National. The road eventually leads on to the small town of Cluny.

Cluny
Whilst it may not appear to play an important role in the current world of wine, this has not always been the case. Little remains of the great Abbey, which was once the head-quarters of the Benedictine order, and which had been responsible for much of the early vineyard planting in Burgundy.

Cluny is on the western fringes of the vineyard area, which broadly lies in the triangle between Cluny and two towns lying on the river Saône, Tournus and Mâcon.

Saints and churches
Tournus is best known for the magnificent church of St. Philibert, where there are the remains not just of that saint, but also of St. Valerian, who was martyred for his faith in the 2nd century. One thing that gives him a particular, if not peculiar, distinction is that after his head had been cut off, he picked it up and walked away with it. In Tournus there is also a gallery dedicated to the painter Jean-Baptiste Greuze (1725–1805).

For those interested in ecclesiastical architecture, the area is particularly known for its Romanesque churches, largely dating back to the 12th century. Those of Donzy and Blanot are particularly beautiful. Just north of Cluny is the village of Taizé, center of a worldwide ecumenical youth movement.

The Mâconnais is not solely dedicated to the production of wine. To the west of Mâcon is the town of Charolles, which has given its name to the well-known breed of cattle, the Charolais. There are also many herds of goats.

Historically the region was known for its red wines made from the Gamay and Pinot Noir grapes. Now most of the production is in white wine, from the Chardonnay. As this is a region of polyculture, most of the growers take their grapes to the local co-operative cellar, of which there seems to be one in nearly every village. Many of these have tasting cellars for the promotion of their wines to passing tourists.

Mâcon-Villages
Much of the wine from the peripheral vineyards in the area has a right only to the simple *appellation*

"Mâcon." In the heart of the area, though, there are 36 villages which have the right to sell their wine either as Mâcon-Villages, or by attaching the village name to Mâcon, such as Mâcon-Lugny or Mâcon-Viré. Two of the villages have given their names to grape varieties, Chasselas and Chardonnay, while one of them, Milly, has added the name of its most famous son, the poet Lamartine.

To visit the vineyards of the Mâcon-Villages, a simple route would be to leave Tournus by the D56 and drive through Chardonnay and Lugny. From there one takes the D82 and the D85 to Igé and La-Roche-Vineuse. After a brief detour to Milly-Lamartine, where the poet lost a fortune in making wine, you can take the main N79 road into Mâcon.

An alternative, and slightly shorter, route would be from Chardonnay to Uchizy, Viré and Clessé, arriving in Mâcon from the north. Either way gives a pleasant pastoral drive through a gentle, rolling landscape.

Value for money

Now that many of the white wines of Burgundy have become very expensive, it is worthwhile looking at those from the Mâconnais. These are made from the same grape, the Chardonnay, and they bear a family resemblance to their rather more aristocratic cousins from Chablis and the Côte d'Or.

It is in areas such as this that real discoveries are to be made, for, apart from the larger co-operatives, there are a number of smaller growers who are justifiably proud of what they make.

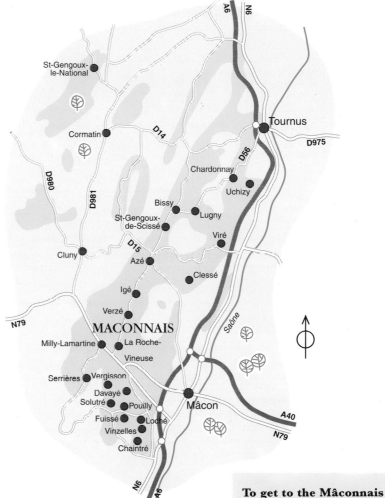

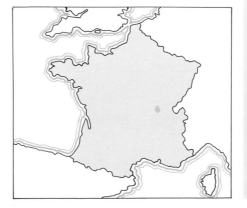

To get to the Mâconnais
Tournus is 53km (33 miles) from Beaune and 364km (266 miles) from Paris by the A6. Mâcon is 83km (52 miles) from Beaune and 395km (247 miles) from Paris.

WINE FESTIVALS
Mâcon Concours des Vins de la St. Vincent, nearest Sat to 22 Jan, Exhibition Center. French National Wine Fair, about 20 May (10 days).
Lugny Haut Mâconnais Wine Fair, Sat before Palm Sun.

MACON
**Maison Mâconnaise
des Vins** ave Maréchal de
Lattre de Tassigny, 71000
Mâcon. Tel: 03 85 38 62 22.
Fax: 03 85 38 82 20. Every
day 0800-2100. Shop
1000-1900. Light meals.
TF.WS.E. (☎ for groups).

VINZELLES
**Cave des Grands Crus
Blancs** 71680 Vinzelles.
Tel: 03 85 35 61 88. Fax:
03 85 35 60 43. Every day
0800-1230, 1400-1930.
TF.WS.

FOR FURTHER INFORMATION
B.I.V.B. 520 ave
Maréchal de Lattre de
Tassigny, 71000 Mâcon.
Tel: 03 85 38 20 15. Fax:
03 85 38 82 20.
E-mail: bivb@wanadoo.fr
www.bivb.com

*The village and vineyards of
Fuissé huddle together in a natural
amphitheater. Full-bodied rich
white wines are produced in this
sun-trap.*

Greatest Wines of the Mâconnais

To the west and south of Mâcon are the vineyards of Pouilly-Fuissé and its satellites, Pouilly-Vinzelles, Pouilly-Loché and Saint-Véran.

Here, a combination of soil, exposure of the vineyards and climate go to create white burgundies with their own character. While still dry, they have a soft richness that makes them very appealing, and they have a particularly strong following in the U.S.

Pouilly-Fuissé is the most famous of these wines, and has been very successful despite its hard-to-pronounce name. Although sweet wines are not typical of the area, they are occasionally made in very hot years.

Mâcon

These vineyards lie on the doorstep of Mâcon, a beautiful town despite the fact that its buildings have suffered badly over the centuries. It is the administrative capital for the region and its wines. It has had a wine fair since the first half of the 14th century and, since 1933, has held the annual French National Wine Fair, where wines from all over France and often further afield can be tasted for a nominal sum.

For the motorist hurrying down the motorway to the beaches of the Mediterranean or the Alpine ski-slopes, Mâcon can make a convenient halt, with its many fine restaurants and hotels.

If there is no time to visit the neighboring vineyards, a full range of the local wines can be tasted, with or without a light meal, at the Maison des Vins, on the way into the town from the north.

A famous crag

The vineyard skyline of Pouilly-Fuissé is dominated by two dramatic crags, the rocks of Vergisson and Solutré. For some reason that I have never discovered, that of Vergisson appears to have played no role whatsoever in history, while that of Solutré has a colorful legend attached to it. This recounts that prehistoric people used to drive herds of horses to their death over the edge.

The truth is more prosaic. The human settlement was located at the foot of the precipice, and it is this that accounts for the mounds of animal bones found there.

Pouilly-Fuissé

The vineyards of Pouilly-Fuissé are in a natural amphitheater of vines spread between the four villages of Vergisson, Solutré, Fuissé and Chaintré. The wines are all dry and white, though they have a deep richness of body that is not found elsewhere in Burgundy. I do not know whether it is this or the name that appeals to the American consumer, but, because of the small production and the enormous demand, the wines of Pouilly-Fuissé tend to be expensive.

Fortunately, the adaptability of the Burgundian producers has created a small number of alternative, if lesser, wines from the same region. The production of two of these, Pouilly-Loché and Pouilly-Vinzelles, is quite small, but about 20 years ago, the new *appellation* of Saint-Véran was created to satisfy some of the demand.

This wine comes from a small number of villages surrounding the vineyards of Pouilly-Fuissé. Some of them formerly made, and still can make, Mâcon-Villages; the others make Beaujolais blanc, for here the vineyards of the Beaujolais and the Mâconnais overlap.

Vineyard circuit

The circuit of these vineyards of the southern Mâconnais is short and simple, though rather winding. Leave Mâcon by the D54 and shortly after passing under the motorway, fork right to Davayé, where there is the local wine school, and Vergisson.

On the far side of the village, you turn left and drive round the back of the rock of Solutré to the village of the same name.

From Solutré, the road leads to Pouilly and the picturesque village of Fuissé, where there is a sign saying, "A hundred growers bid you welcome." Some of the best wine comes from the Château de Fuissé. From here there is a narrow lane down to Loché and Vinzelles, but it is probably easier to drive round via Chaintré. Here the choice is either a return to Mâcon or an attack on the Beaujolais.

The vineyards of Pouilly-Fuissé are dominated by the rock of Solutré.

The Beaujolais

A cellarman in Villié-Morgon studies a glass of the cru Beaujolais, Morgon. Behind him on the barrel-head is what looks like a watering can. This is used for topping up the wine barrels.

For many wine lovers, the Beaujolais is the most enjoyable of all wine regions. It has a relaxed atmosphere that is all its own. It is a place where the importance of time seems to be eternally diminished and thus it is the wrong place for those who want to break away from the motorway just to gain a small sample of its flavor.

The flavor of the Beaujolais is not just its wine or its countryside – a succession of rounded hills leading ultimately to the beginnings of the Massif Central. It is the red-roofed villages round the squares where the click of *boules* is rivalled by the clink of bottle on glass at the tables outside the welcoming bars.

A wine to be enjoyed

Beaujolais, as a wine, does not seek to be taken too seriously. It is there to be enjoyed, and if it is difficult to prove the local claim that Beaujolais is the only wine that can quench a thirst,

there is every incentive to put it to the test by taking another glass ... and another.

Even with detailed instructions, it is easy to get lost, for the contours do not permit straight roads, and in any case they might speed up the pace of life.

The *Clochemerle* novels of Gabriel Chevalier are not an exaggeration of that life in the Beaujolais, but rather a loving look at it.

Geography of the Beaujolais

Broadly speaking, the Beaujolais can be divided into two parts. In the south, beyond Villefranche-sur-Saône is the Bas-Beaujolais. Here the soil is largely sandy, and lighter, earlier-maturing wines are made; most of those wines that we see as Beaujolais Nouveau.

In the north, between Mâcon and Villefranche, the soil is more granitic. From here come the fuller, fruitier wines of the Beaujolais-Villages and the ten *crus*, those villages that can sell their wine just under their own names.

Throughout the region, the red wines are made with just one grape, the Gamay. This is despised in the rest of Burgundy, but in the Beaujolais it is king.

Alternative routes

The main road, the N6, skirts the eastern fringes of the Beaujolais vineyards. While the villages along it may house many of the most important wine merchants of the region, and while there may be the occasional tasting cellar to cause the hurried motorist to halt for a while, to taste and perhaps to buy, this is not the Beaujolais.

Seventy years ago, two local writers, Léon Foillard and Tony David, suggested a three-day circuit by

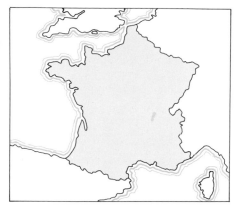

To get to the Beaujolais
Villefranche-sur-Saône is
439km (274 miles) from
Paris and 31km (20 miles)
from Lyon on the A6.

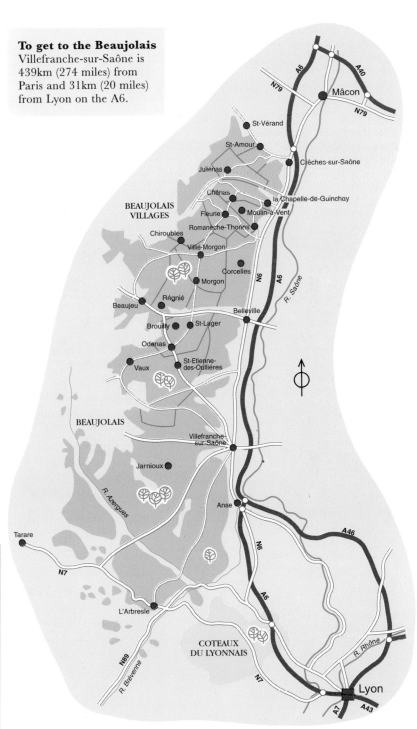

car in the Beaujolais. The modern
alternative is a choice of three
different Beaujolais "routes," which
are clearly marked. Two of these lie
between Mâcon and Villefranche,
whilst the third, *au pays des pierres dorées*,
meanders round the southern part of
the region.

With the modern motorist in mind
there is also a "fast" route, which turns
off the N6 at Crêches-sur-Saône, 8km
(5 miles) south of Mâcon, and leads
through the famous *crus* beginning
with Saint-Amour, then Juliénas,
where there is a beautiful château,
largely rebuilt at the beginning of the
18th century, and the earlier arcaded
Maison de la Dîme, where church
tithes were collected.

The Charter of Villefranche

The "capital" of the Beaujolais is
Villefranche, which is a convenient,
if noisy, base from which to tour the
region. It benefits from a 68-article
charter dating from 1260.

Among other things, this states
that a husband can only be punished
for striking his wife if she dies as a
result, while the penalty for being
caught in adultery is to run naked
through the streets – or pay a fine.

The Château de la Chaize at Odenas is one of the most beautiful properties in the Beaujolais. The property's vineyards produce an excellent Brouilly.

BEAUJEU
S.C.I. Pavillon de Chavannes
Chavannes, Quincié,
69430 Beaujeu. Tel:
04 74 04 35 01. Fax:
04 74 69 01 09. Mon-Fri
1400-1800. TF.WS.E.S. ☎
E-mail: pauljambon@aol.com

BROUILLY
**Mme La Marquise de
Roussy de Sales** Château
de la Chaize, Odenas, 69460
St. Etienne-des-Oullières.
Tel: 04 74 03 41 05. Fax:
04 74 03 52 73. (Mme
Martray). Mon-Fri 0800-
1200, 1330-1800. Closed
Aug, Christmas and Easter.
TP.WS.E. ☎ E-mail: chateau
delachaize@ wanadoo.fr

MORGON LES CHARMES
Domaine des Pillets les
Pillets, 69910 Villié-Morgon.
Tel: 04 74 04 21 60. Fax:
04 74 69 15 28. (M. Gérard
Brisson). Mon-Sat 0900-
1200, 1400-1800. Closed
first 10 days in Aug.
TF.WS.E.G. ☎
E-mail: gerard.brisson@
wanadoo.fr

MOULIN-A-VENT
Château des Jacques
71570 Romanèche-Thorins.
Tel: 03 85 35 51 64. Fax:
03 85 35 59 15. Mon-Sun
0900-1830. TF.WS.E. ☎
www.louisjadot.com
Château Portier
Moulin-à-Vent, Romanèche-
Thorins, 71570 La
Chapelle-de-Guinchay.
Tel: 03 85 35 51 57. Fax:
03 80 22 08 91. Mon-Fri
0800-1200, 1400-1800.
Closed Aug. Range of *crus*
and red, rosé and white
Beaujolais. TF (with
purchase). WS. ☎

Moulin-à-Vent, Fleurie and Morgon

Within the boundaries of Chénas is the sole windmill of the Beaujolais, but perhaps one of the best known in the world, for it has given its name to the wine Moulin-à-Vent.

From Fleurie the route goes to Villié-Morgon and the hamlet of Morgon, from where it is worth making a short diversion to the left to visit the beautiful Château de Pizay.

Brouilly

Saint-Lager lies at the foot of the Mont de Brouilly, at the top of which is a small chapel, Notre-Dame du Raisin, the object of a well-refreshed pilgrimage each year on 8 September. There is a road to the top, from where there is a magnificent view of the Beaujolais vineyards.

Odenas

At Odenas is the Château de la Chaize, built at the end of the 17th century by the nephew of the confessor of Louis XIV. The gardens were designed by Le Nôtre and the cellar is a national monument, the longest single vaulted cellar in the Beaujolais. From there the rapid route passes through Saint-Etienne-des-Oullières to Villefranche.

The *route touristique*

The *route touristique* follows largely the same outline but with a number of diversions. The first takes in the Château de Corcelles, which is open to the public.

The second is the former capital of the region, Beaujeu, which like Beaune has a hospital financed in part by its vineyard holdings.

The Château also owns La Grange Chartron at Régnié, which was built as an immense vineyard estate building at the beginning of the last century.

Régnié also has the distinction of being the last village to have its wines elevated to *cru* status. The final diversion takes in Vaux, the village that was the model for the *Clochemerle* books.

Les pierres dorées

The *pierres dorées* or "golden stones" circuit wanders vaguely for some 50 km (30 miles). Here the main attractions are the beautiful scenery, the castles at Jarnioux and Châtillon d'Azergues and a liberal selection of tasting cellars, many attached to co-operative cellars.

Tasting cellars and restaurants

There is no shortage of opportunity to taste the wines of the Beaujolais. Round every corner there seems to be a tasting cellar. There are also many fine restaurants specializing in the simple, but hearty, food of the neighborhood. Here the motto could be, "Eat, drink and be merry" with no thought for tomorrow.

The village of Fleurie has a fine reputation for its charcuterie as well as its wine. Indeed, the co-operative cellar was founded by Monsieur Chabert, who combined the roles of pork butcher and vigneron.

FOOD IN BURGUNDY

The diversity of the wines of Burgundy is matched by the diversity of its foods, and wine sauces form an essential part of the cookery, be it the white wines, for dishes like *Jambon* (ham) *au Chablis*, or the reds for *Coq au Chambertin* or *Oeufs en Meurette*.

Close at hand, too, is the city of Lyon, whose restaurants are renowned throughout the world of fine food. A local saying has it that it is watered by three rivers, the Rhône, the Saône, and the Beaujolais!

Burgundy is rich in its raw materials. The river Saône and its tributaries provide plenty of coarse fish for such traditional dishes as the *Pochouse* of Verdun sur le Doubs. From beyond the river come Bresse chickens, with their distinctive yellowish flesh and rich texture, from their diet of maize. There are also the waterfowl of the Dombes.

Charolais beef gives magnificent steaks and the base for that dish that never seems to succeed so well elsewhere, *Boeuf Bourguignon*. The forests of the Morvan and the Châtillonnais offer venison and wild boar to go with the fullest-bodied wines of the Côte de Nuits.

The snails of Burgundy, too, are without rival, though their collection is now strictly limited.

Finally, Burgundy is proud of its cheeses. From north-west of Dijon comes Epoisses, often aged in the local brandy. The monks of Cîteaux make a tangy cow's-milk cheese. Goat's-milk cheeses are also made throughout the region, perhaps the best-known being the Chevreton de Mâcon. However, if you can find it, try the rare Claquebitou of the Hautes-Côtes.

ROMANECHE-THORINS
Le Hameau en Beaujolais 71570 Romanèche-Thorins. Tel: 03 85 35 22 22. Fax: 03 85 35 21 18. Every day 0900-1830. This is a wine "theme park" established by Beaujolais producer Georges Duboeuf. T.F.WS.E.G.I.S. www.hameau.du.vin.tm.fr
ST. ETIENNE-LA-VARENNE
Château des Tours 69460 St.-Etienne-la-Varenne. Tel: 04 74 03 40 86. Fax: 04 74 03 50 22. Mon-Fri 0800-1200, 1400-1800. T.F.WS.E. (☎ Mon-Fri) (☎ Sat, Sun).
SALLES-ARBUISSONNAS-EN-BEAUJOLAIS
Domaine Christian Miolane E.A.R.L. La Folie, 69460 Salles-Arbuissonnas. Tel: 04 74 67 52 67 or 04 74 60 52 48. Fax: 04 74 67 59 95. Mon-Sat by appointment only. Audio-visual presentation, collection of wine implements. TF (with purchase). WS.D.E. ☎

The Rhône

FOR FURTHER INFORMATION
Inter Rhône
6, rue des 3 Faucons,
84024 Avignon.
Tel: 04 90 27 24 00.
Fax: 04 90 27 24 13.

Amongst the finest vineyards producing Côtes-du-Rhône-Villages lies the 12th-century château of Suze-la-Rousse. Here has been established the Université du Vin, *which gives courses on the wines of France throughout the year.*

Since before Roman times, the valley of the Rhône has been one of the great highways of the civilized world. As with many highways, most who pass along it are mainly interested in reaching their destination and pay little heed to what is on either side. The wines of the Rhône, however, deserve more attention for their individuality and quality. The Rhône is one of the greatest wine rivers of the world. Near its source, in Switzerland, are produced the sensational wines of the Valais. After it leaves Lake Geneva and flows westward, it passes through Savoy where the sparkling wines of Seyssel are made. However it is only after it joins the Saône at Lyon and turns southward that it concerns us in this chapter.

In the next 230km (143 miles), as far as Avignon, some of the finest wines in the world are made; wines such as Côte Rôtie and Hermitage, Tavel and Muscat de Beaumes-de-Venise.

There are three main roads down the valley of the Rhône. On the west bank there is the N86, on the east the N7, and then the motorway, the A7.

Of these three roads, it is the first that is the route of the dedicated vineyard visitor, for driving south from Lyon it is on that side of the river that he will find all the well-known vineyards as far as Tournon. It is not, however, a fast road and, if your time is limited, it is probably better to use the motorway and take the most convenient exit for the vineyards you want to see: Vienne South for Côte-Rôtie and Condrieu; Tournon for Hermitage; and Orange for Châteauneuf-du-Pape.

While the Rhône valley is perhaps best known for its full-bodied red wines, the area does produce a surprising selection and variety. As well as reds, there are also fine dry white wines (in the 19th century, white Hermitage was considered to be one of the great wines of the world), excellent rosés such as Tavel and Lirac, sparkling wine from Saint-Péray and luscious sweet wines, such as the Muscats of Beaumes-de-Venise.

There is one wine that is produced along almost the full length of the vineyards, and that is simple Côtes-du-Rhône. For the most part this is red wine, though white and rosé wines are also made. The most common grape variety is Grenache, but others are used as necessary.

Vienne

The town of Vienne lies some 30km (19 miles) south of Lyon, and it is just south of here that the Rhône vineyards begin. Vienne is one of the oldest cities of France, dating back to long before Roman times. There are the remains of a temple dedicated to the Emperor Augustus and his wife Livia and there is a tradition that Hannibal left the Rhône valley here on his trans-Alpine journey. Vienne played an important role in early Christian history and one can still read the Epistle of the Martyrs of Vienne to their colleagues in the eastern Church.

Côte Rôtie

Just south of Vienne, on the other bank of the river, are the vineyards of Côte Rôtie. These are among the steepest in France and the vines are planted in a unique fashion: three separate vines on individual poles that meet together at the top.

The two main slopes are called the Côte Brune and the Côte Blonde, in memory of the two beautiful daughters of a local nobleman. Most Côte Rôtie is a blend from the two sources. At the foot of the vineyards is the town of Ampuis, home to many of the growers and merchants.

To get to the Rhône
Vienne is 490km (306 miles) from Paris and 92km (57 miles) from Mâcon on the A6 and A7 motorways. Orange is 657km (410 miles) from Paris and 259km (162 miles) from Mâcon.

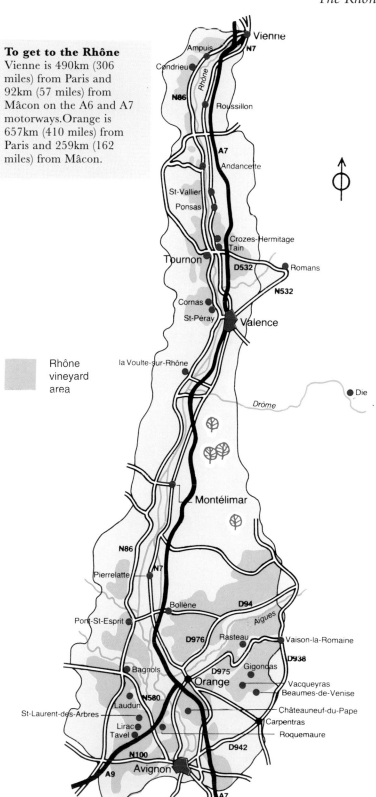

Rhône vineyard area

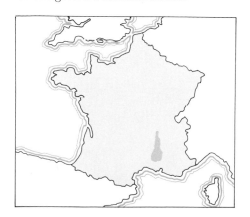

CONDRIEU
Georges Vernay 1, rte Nationale, 69420 Condrieu. Tel: 04 74 59 52 22. Fax: 04 74 56 60 98. (M. Luc Vernay). Every day 0900-1200, 1430-1900. TP.WS.E.I. ☎ www.georges-vernay.fr

CHATEAU GRILLET
Neyret-Gachet Château Grillet, 42410 Verin. Tel: 04 74 59 51 56. Fax: 04 78 92 96 10. By appointment only. WS.E. ☎

COTE ROTIE
S.A.J. Vidal-Fleury rte Nationale, 69420 Ampuis. Tel: 04 74 56 10 18. Fax: 04 74 56 19 19. (M. Regnier-Vigouroux). Mon-Thu 0800-1200, 1400-1800 (1700 Fri). Closed at weekends and holidays. TF (TP for groups). WS.E. ☎

ST JOSEPH
Cave St Désirat 07340 St Désirat. Tel: 04 75 34 22 05. Fax: 04 75 34 30 10. (M. Chaleat). Every day 0800-1200, 1400-1900. Audio-visual presentation, picnic area. TF.WS.E. www.cave-saint.desirat.com

Condrieu

Five km (3 miles) further along the road from Côte Rôtie comes the village of Condrieu, renowned for its long-lasting white wine of the same name, made from the Viognier grape. At one time this was found almost nowhere else in the world, but this short stretch of the Rhône valley, although in recent years it has been planted extensively in Languedoc.

Château Grillet

The Viognier reaches its peak in the wines of Château Grillet, a vineyard, which has its own microclimate and the smallest production of any single *appellation contrôlée* in France. The rarity of both Condrieu and Château Grillet means that they are not cheap, but their individual, luscious, sunny, fruity, yet dry, flavor should not be missed.

Ardèche

On the western bank of the river come the almost entirely red wines of Saint-Joseph, made from the Syrah grape.

We are now in the Ardèche *département* and it is here that many experimental plantings have been made with "foreign" grapes such as the Gamay and the Chardonnay. The famous Burgundy house of Louis Latour, for example, has planted in the region, because of the comparative cheapness of the land and the favorable climate. Because the wines are not made from the traditional grape varieties, they do not have *appellation contrôlée* status, but that of *vin de pays*. Many of these are of excellent quality.

On the other bank of the river is the town of Saint-Vallier, which was once a center of the silk trade. Just to the south, the village of Ponsas is overlooked by a rocky cliff, called Pilate's Castle, as the legend has it that Pontius Pilate committed suicide by jumping off it.

Hermitage

No one would claim that the twin towns of Tain and Tournon are attractive,

The steep hillside vineyard of one of the greatest red wines of France, Côte Rôtie, originally planted in Roman times. One of the major owners is the company of Etienne Guigal, based in the nearby town of Ampuis.

but above them rises the stark hillside famous for Hermitage wine. There have been vines planted here for more than two thousand years, despite Celtic claims that they were first planted by St Patrick. The hill gets its name, however, from Gaspard de Stérimberg, who retired to a cell on the summit, having been wounded after fighting the Albigensian heretics in 1224.

There are two distinct types of soil on the hill: granitic for the red grapes, and clayey for the white. The exposure to the sun ensures that exceptionally full-bodied wines are made, which are capable of lasting for decades.

Traditionally, there are a number of differently named sites on the hill, each giving a wine with its individual character. Occasionally, these can be found as individual wines, but more often they are blended together to produce the perfect whole.

Crozes-Hermitage and Cornas

Eleven villages surrounding the hill of Hermitage have the right to call their wine Crozes-Hermitage. While there is a relationship in style with its illustrious neighbor, it is not as close as the growers would have you believe; the reds might age well, but the whites are certainly best drunk young.

Returning to the other side of the river, opposite the important town of Valence, there are two small areas producing fine wines. The first of these is Cornas. Again, the vineyards are on steep slopes and the combination of soil and microclimate

Whilst the Rhône valley is particularly known for its red wines, it also produces some excellent white wines. Of these, the rarest and most expensive is Château Grillet, made from the Viognier grape.

Nougat being prepared in copper vessels at Suprême Nougat. (3, ave St Martin, 26200 Montélimar. Tel: 04 75 01 74 42. Open to visitors.)

BEAUMES-DE-VENISE

Vignerons de Beaumes de Venise Quartier Ravel, 84190 Beaumes-de-Venise. Tel: 04 90 12 41 00. Fax: 04 90 65 02 05. Mon-Thu 0800-1200, 1400-1800 (1700 Fri). TF.WS.E.

GIGONDAS

E.A.R.L, J.P. and M. Meffre Domaine St Gayan, 84190 Gigondas. Tel: 04 90 65 86 33. Fax: 04 90 65 85 10. (M. or Mme Meffre). Every day 0900-1145, 1400-1900. TF.WS. (☎ Sun.) www.club-internet.fr/perso/jpmeffre

gives perhaps the biggest wine of the Rhône. As one English writer has said, "A good Cornas one or two years old is a savage, dark wine that leaves the eye impressed and the palate colored."

Two sparkling wine areas

The reputation of the wines of Saint-Péray goes back to classical times. Traditionally still and white, four-fifths are now sparkling, made in the same way as Champagne. Murray's *Handbook for France*, dated 1884, suggests that the visitor to Valence should "Try here the sparkling wine of St Péray, an excellent wine, not inferior to Champagne, 3 or 4fr the bottle." The price may have changed, but not the quality.

The other sparkling wine area is around Die, some 65km (40 miles) away on the other side of the Rhône, on one of its tributaries, the Drôme. Here two styles of wine are made: a *brut* (Crémant de Die) by the traditional champagne method, and

a sweeter variety (Clairette de Die) where the sparkle in the bottle comes from a naturally delayed first fermentation.

Coteaux de Tricastin

After Valence, there is a break in the vineyards of the Rhône lasting some 70km (43 miles). It is not until after Montélimar, renowned for its nougat, that, on the left bank of the Rhône, begin the vineyards of the Coteaux de Tricastin.

Here the land is stony and poor, continually scoured by the Mistral, and it is only in the last 30 years that vines have been replanted since they were destroyed by phylloxera. Much of the planting has been carried out by *pieds noirs* (ex-colonials from Algeria). The wines, mainly red, are very similar to Côtes du Rhône.

Orange

Beyond the riverside nuclear power-station at Pierrelatte, the vineyards producing Côtes du Rhône begin again and it is from the three départements of Drôme, Vaucluse and Gard that the bulk of it comes. At the center of the region is the town of Orange, the scene of an annual wine fair, held in the Roman amphitheater.

For many years, Orange was the capital of a small independent principality, which was not integrated into France until the Treaty of Utrecht in 1713. It also gave its name to William of Orange. Remains include a Roman triumphal arch on the northern side of the town and traces of a Roman circus.

Gigondas and Vacqueyras

To the north-east lie a number of villages that have traditionally sold their wine as simple Côtes du Rhône, or the superior Côtes du Rhône Villages. Some of these have progressed above this status.

Gigondas, where there are the remains of a castle that belonged to the Princes of Orange, had the good fortune to be the home of two wine merchants intent on promoting the local wines and in 1971 was rewarded with full *appellation contrôlée* status for its red wines.

Vacqueyras, its neighbor, has since followed in its footsteps. Rasteau, on the other hand, has built its reputation on a fortified wine made in the same way as port, but from the Grenache grape.

Beaumes-de-Venise

Better known is the Muscat de Beaumes-de-Venise. Beaumes-de-Venise was a spa in Roman times and has been well known for its wines for many centuries. No one for sure knows when the Muscat grape was first planted here. It is the only place where it can be found in the entire Rhône valley.

However, there is every possibility that the Greeks, who settled along the Mediterranean coast before the Romans, also used Beaumes-de-Venise as a spa, and brought the grape – a firm favorite of theirs – with them. Certainly its rich fruitiness seems to have had a wider appeal than most other wines of its type made in France.

VACQUEYRAS
Caves des Vignerons de Vacqueyras 84190 Vacqueyras. Tel: 04 90 65 84 54. Fax: 04 90 65 81 32. Every day 0900-1200, 1400-1800. TF.WS.E.G.S. ☎ www.vins-du-troubadour.tm.fr
Domaine de Fourmone rte de Bollène, 84190 Vacqueyras. Tel: 04 90 65 86 05. Fax: 04 90 65 87 84. Every day 0900-1200, 1400-1800. TF.WS.E. ☎

Among the delights of the Rhône vineyards are the sweet wines made from the Muscat grape, particularly around Beaumes-de-Venise. Here, the overripe grapes are being picked.

Overlooking the vineyards of Gigondas and Vacqueyras is Mont Ventoux. Along its southern slopes run the vineyards of Côtes du Ventoux. A little white wine is made, but most of the production is of a soft, easy drinking red wine.

Châteauneuf-du-Pape

Orange is one of the five communes which together produce perhaps the best-known wine of the Rhône valley, Châteauneuf-du-Pape. There is no doubt that much of the historic reputation of this wine is due to the fact that when the Popes left Rome and established themselves in nearby Avignon during the 14th century they did much to promote the local wines. It was at Châteauneuf that they built their summer palace and there are still some remains of this.

The complexity of the wine of Châteauneuf is due largely to the fact that up to 13 different grape varieties may be used in its production, each adding a touch of color to the final picture. The soil is closely covered with large rounded stones and the closely pruned vines benefit from an inverted form of night storage heating: the stones retain through the night much of the heat that they have picked up during the day, and pass it on to the vines.

The local growers have been in the forefront of supporting legislation to protect the quality of their wines. Many of them, in a form of regional pride, have adopted a special bottle, bearing the papal coat of arms on its shoulder.

Châteauneuf is best known for its red wines, which are full-bodied and capable of long ageing, but it also produces small quantities of an excellent white wine.

Avignon

The history of Avignon is closely linked to the period during which seven Popes, and three anti-Popes, lived there. The church purchased the city by some rather sharp practice. Joanna of Naples, who was still a minor, was persuaded to sell it for the sum of 80,000 gold crowns. Rather sadly, she never received the money, though the Popes had already taken possession of the city. When the Popes returned to Rome, it remained part of their possessions, being governed by a Papal Legate. Indeed, it did not finally become part of France until after the French Revolution.

Having had as many as 80,000 inhabitants during the 17th century, the population was less than half that a hundred years ago. It is only quite recently that it has returned to its previous glory.

The mobile stills that used to travel from village to village in France to distill spirits from grapes and other fruit are, sadly, on the decline. Here is a retired example, from Châteauneuf-du-Pape, built in 1920.

CHATEAUNEUF-DU-PAPE
Henry Bouachon – Les Caves Saint Pierre ave Pierre de Luxembourg, 84230 Châteauneuf-du-Pape. Tel: 04 90 83 58 35. Fax: 04 90 83 77 23. Summer Mon-Fri 0830-1200, 1400-1730. TF.WS.E.G.S. ☎ (☎ for groups). www.henry.bouachon.com
Château Mont-Redon rte D68, 84230 Châteauneuf-du-Pape. Tel: 04 90 83 72 75. Fax: 04 90 83 77 20. Every day 0800-1900. TF.WS.E. www.chateaumontredon.fr
Domaine-La-Roquette 2, ave Louis Pasteur, 84230 Châteauneuf-du-Pape. Tel: 04 90 33 00 31. Fax: 04 90 33 18 47. Apr-Sep, Mon-Fri 0900-1200, 1400-1800. TF.WS.E.
Paul Avril Clos des Papes, 84230 Châteauneuf-du-Pape. Tel: 04 90 83 70 13. Fax: 04 90 83 50 87. (Mme Nicolai). Mon-Fri 0900-1130, 1400-1700. TF.WS.E.I. ☎ (☎ for groups).

There is much to see in Avignon. It is still surrounded by 14th-century battlements with 39 watch towers. The former Palace of the Popes has been at various times a military barracks and even a prison. This must have been a great come-down from the days of luxurious extravagance and debauchery that marked the times of the Papal court.

Sur le pont....

Dancing on the bridge at Avignon, or at least on the 800-year-old Pont Saint Bénézet, is now strictly limited, as only four out of the original 19 arches remain. On it, there is the small chapel of St Nicolas, which holds the remains of the saint who gave the bridge his name.

Behind the church of St Didier, the narrow Rue du Roi René has a number of beautiful old buildings.

To the north-west of Avignon are the Côtes du Rhône vineyards of the Gard *département*. These are particularly known for their rosé wines. The west bank of the Rhône, here, presents a totally different outlook to the east. Instead of a picture of rich greens, there is the drab grey aridity of the *garrigues* (areas of rough, stony countryside) baked by the sun and tormented by the wind. The soil is basically chalky, but is covered by layers of flat, flaking stones, which, as in Châteauneuf, reflect the heat.

Two of the villages, Chusclan and Laudun, have the *appellation* Côtes du Rhône Villages, but two others, Tavel and Lirac, have their own individual *appellations*.

Tavel has long had the reputation of producing the finest rosé wine in France. In Britain and the United States, where the consumption of

rosé wine represents only a small fraction of the total, this may not appear a very important title, but in France, where a lot is drunk, Tavel is held in high esteem.

Much of the vineyard area was allowed to return to scrubland after the phylloxera plague, and it is only during the last thirty years or so that the vineyards of Tavel have taken on

The typical Rhône vineyard village of Gigondas, with its flattened red-tiled roofs. Here are produced full-bodied, warming red wines.

AIGUES-MORTES
Domaines Listel
Domaine de Jarras, 30220
Aigues-Mortes. Tel:
04 66 51 17 00. Fax:
04 66 51 17 29. Easter-15
Oct, every day 1000-1800.
15 Oct-Easter, Mon-Fri
0900-1130, 1400-1730.
Historic cellars, video,
picnic area. TF.WS.E.
(☎ for groups).
CHUSCLAN
**Caves des Vignerons
de Chusclan** 30200
Chusclan. Tel: 04 66 90 11 03.
Fax: 04 66 90 16 52.
(M. Theraroz). Mon-Sun
0800-1200, 1400-1830.
Collection of wine
implements, picnic area.
TF.WS.E.
COSTIERES DE NIMES
**Chantal and Pierre-Yves
Comte** Château de la
Tuilerie, rte de St Gilles,
30900 Nîmes. Tel: 04 66 70
07 52. Fax: 04 66 70 04 36.

*On the west bank of the Rhône,
the historic port of Roquemaure
lies in the center of the
appellation of Lirac.*

a new lease of life with extensive
replanting. Much of the initiative for
this has come from the local co-
operative, which has the reputation
of being one of the most dynamic
and conscientious in France.

Wine from Lirac
Four villages have the right to make
Lirac wine. Of these, Saint-Laurent-
des-Arbres is perhaps the most
attractive, with an early fortified
church. Roquemaure, too, has a long
history, claiming a supporting role in
the Hannibal story.

Castles in the air
Whilst Lirac was best known for its
rosé wines, an ever-increasing
quantity of red wine is now being
made. Regular attenders at French
wine fairs, the Pons-Mure family
came to the region after Algerian
independence. Not having a château
to put on their labels, they decided
to call their wine Castel Oualou,
which, I gather, is Arabic for the
castle that does not exist or, perhaps,
castle in the air. To complete the
image, they added some turrets

straight out of Walt Disney. This did
not appeal to the sense of humor of the
local authorities and they asked for the
picture to be removed. Instead, the
family put a cross over the fairy-tale
castle – and that is how the labels look
to this day.

The Pont du Gard
It is about here that the vineyards of
the Côte du Rhône finish, but one short
excursion that is well worth making
from Avignon is to the Pont du Gard.
This is some 22km (14 miles) west of
the town, beyond Remoulins on the
N100. The Pont is a magnificent
Roman aqueduct, in three tiers, 48
meters (160 feet) above the valley of the
river Gardon. The channel to carry the
water is more than 2 meters (7 feet)
deep and over a meter (4 feet) wide. Just
20km (12.5 miles) further on is the
magnificent city of Nîmes.

While we have come to the end of
the vineyards of the Côtes du Rhône,
there are still what might be called
some "Rhône" vineyards in the region
of the Costières de Nîmes, on the
western fringes of the Rhône delta.
Here most of the wine is red, though
there is also some rosé and a little
white. These wines are often good value
for money.

More unusual is the white Clairette
de Bellegarde, from south-east of
Nîmes, which has its own *appellation*

FOOD IN THE RHONE

It is difficult to write about the food specialties of the Rhône, for gastronomically it is not one area. Indeed, whilst driving down it, you cross the great boundary in French gastronomy: on one side the cooking is done with butter and on the other with olive oil.

In the north, Lyon is one of the gastronomic centers of France, known for its sausages, like *rosette* and *judas*, its tripe and dishes like *la poularde demi-deuil*, chicken in cream with truffles.

Down the valley of the Rhône, there are a number of seasonal fruit markets for apricots, nectarines and, near Carpentras, melons. The Ardèche is known for its chestnuts and the Drôme for its herbs, honey and thrush patés. For a sticky finale, the best nougat in the world comes from Montélimar.

contrôlée. The production is very small; the wine is dry, with a flowery flavor and little acidity.

More common, perhaps because the village that gives it its name straddles the main N113 road, is Muscat de Lunel. This, as the name suggests, is a sweet fortified wine made from the muscat grape. It lacks, for the most part, the finesse of flavor that one finds in the similar wines from Beaumes-de-Venise.

The Camargue

Where the river Rhône reaches the Mediterranean, the deposit that it has carried down has created a vast sandy delta, the Camargue, noted for its bulls, horses and flamingoes. This seems the most unlikely place for vineyards to be planted, but it is here that one finds one of the biggest vineyard companies in France, Les Salins du Midi (Listel).

As its name suggests, this company has traditionally made its money from salt; indeed, it still does so. In a bid to diversify and to use land that otherwise would have no commercial application, it has planted along the coast from Sète eastward, almost to the mouth of the Rhône more than 1600 hectares (almost 4000 acres) of vines. Here a broad range of wines is made with the *appellation* of Vin de Pays des Sables du Golfe du Lion. The largest of these properties, the Domaine de Jarras, lies on the main D979 road from Aigues-Mortes to le Grau-du-Roi.

It seems fitting that our journey through the vineyards of the Rhône valley should finish here in the medieval walled town of Aigues-Mortes, for it was from here that St Louis set out on his own pilgrimage, crusades to the Holy Land.

These vineyards at Montcalm in the Camargue have been planted on reclaimed land.

TAVEL
Domaine Maby 30126 Tavel. Tel: 04 66 50 03 40. Fax: 04 66 50 43 12. Mon-Fri 0800-1200, 1400-1800. Closed first fortnight in Aug. TF.WS.

Les Vignerons de Tavel 30126 Tavel. Tel: 04 66 50 03 57. Fax: 04 66 50 46 57. Every day 0800-1200, 1400-1900. TF.WS.E. E-mail: tavel.cave@wanadoo.fr www.tavel.tm.fr

WINE FESTIVALS
Ampuis *Marché aux vins*, third Sat Jan.
Châteauneuf-du-Pape Festival of St Marc, about 25 Apr.
Côte du Rhône Villages Fair alternate years, always in different village.
Cornas Wine Fair first weekend Dec.
Orange Wine Fair Jul and Aug.

The Loire Valley

FOR FURTHER INFORMATION
F.I.V.A.L. 47, rue Jules
Simon, 37000 Tours.
Tel: 02 47 64 48 00.
Fax: 02 47 64 18 19.

It is easy to see why the French kings treated the Loire valley as their playground: the climate is temperate, the landscape soft and beguiling, and much of the land is fertile. There was also plenty of honey-colored limestone with which to build the famous châteaux such as Azay-le-Rideau, Chambord and Chenonceau. The valley remains a wonderful region for visitors to explore its rich historical heritage and to discover the diversity of its wines. The Loire is the climatic border between the frequently cold and wet northern France and the warmer south.

Although they are by no means continuous, the Loire vineyards extend over nearly 850km (530 miles) and so it is far too ambitious to try to visit them all at once. It is best to concentrate on a section at a time, for instance Touraine or Anjou-Saumur or the Pays Nantais.

At 1000km (about 600 miles) long, the Loire is easily the longest river in France. The source is high up in the Massif Central, only 100km (60 miles) from the Mediterranean. The Loire drains two fifths of France and for most of its course is a gentle river, although appearances are deceptive: it is prone to flooding and its currents and sandbanks can be treacherous.

The Upper Loire
The first Loire vineyards are those of the Côtes de Forez and the Côte Roannaise, which are just to the north of St Etienne, not far from Lyon on the river Rhône.

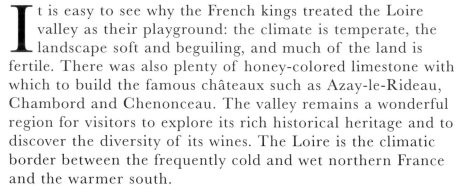

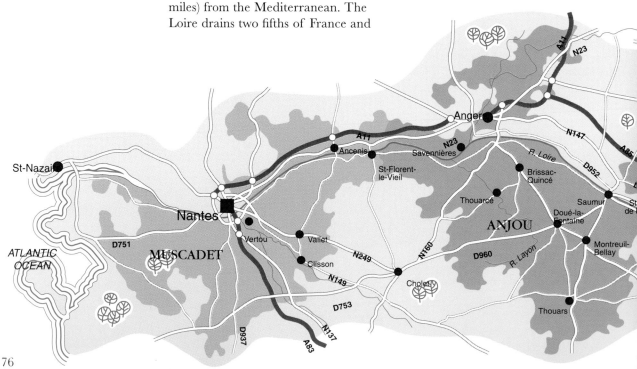

Gamay is the chief variety, and the wines are similar to those of the Beaujolais. Next come those of St Pourçain-sur-Sioule, which are made in three colors from Chardonnay, Tressalier (a local variety), Gamay and Pinot Noir.

All of these vineyards used to be much more important and extensive in the 19th century, as did the Côtes d'Auvergne on the Allier, a tributary to the Loire.

At the end of the last century, there used to be 40,000 hectares (100,000 acres) of vines in the Auvergne; now only 400 hectares (1000 acres) remain. Most these wines are consumed locally. These Upper Loire vineyards are worth visiting if you are in the area but do not warrant a special journey.

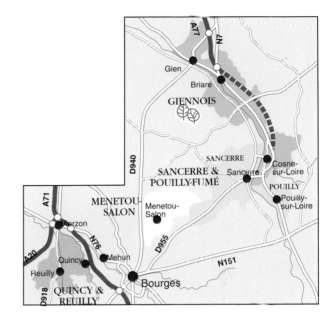

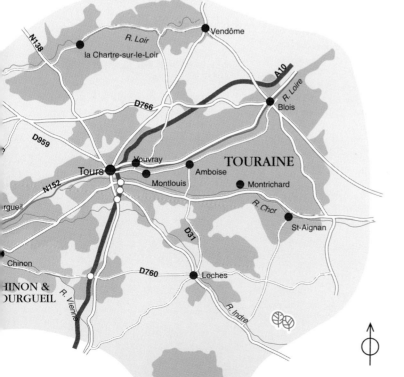

To get to the Loire
From Paris: Tours is 234km (146 miles) by the A10; Angers is 296km (185 miles) and Nantes 380km (237 miles) by the A11. From Calais and Boulogne, Paris can now be avoided by taking the A16, A28 to Rouen and then A13, N154 and A10 to the Loire valley. Tours is 234km (146 miles) from Caen by D514, N158 and N138 and Nantes is 155km (97 miles) from Saint-Malo by the N137.

Central Vineyards

The little town of Pouilly-sur-Loire marks the halfway point of the river Loire and the first appellation with an international reputation. The wines of Pouilly and Sancerre have already been covered in the Burgundy chapter but there are several other appellations in the area that are worth exploring.

Menetou-Salon

Of these Menetou-Salon is the most important and has the most attractive landscape. This appellation adjoins the western limit of Sancerre and produces broadly similar wines from Sauvignon Blanc and Pinot Noir. The area under vines has more than doubled over the past fifteen years with the Menetou-Salon vineyards centered around the two small towns of Morogues and Menetou-Salon.

West of Bourges in the Cher valley are the small appellations of Quincy, with its crisp Sauvignon Blancs, and Reuilly, which makes wine in all three

The village of Chambord boasts one of the most imposing, if not the most beautiful, châteaux of the Loire.

On the river Cher, in the heart of the vineyards of Touraine, lies the village of Pouillé. Here red wines are made from the Cabernet Franc, Côt and Gamay, and whites mainly from the Sauvignon Blanc.

colors. Here the permitted varieties are Sauvignon Blanc, Pinot Gris and Pinot Noir. Well to the south of Bourges are the tiny vineyards of Châteaumeillant with its Gamay and Pinot Noir based wines.

Heading north from Pouilly-sur-Loire, you find the scattered vineyards of the newly promoted Coteaux de Giennois, with wines made from Sauvignon Blanc, Gamay and Pinot Noir. Then around Orléans are the vestiges of the once important vineyards that used to supply Paris. Now only 100 hectares (242 acres) are left, growing Auvernat Blanc (Chardonnay), Auvernat Rouge (Pinot Noir) and Gris Meunier.

Orléans and Vinegar

Orléans was once the port for wines that had come along the Loire and would be unloaded and sent to Paris. It was common for wines to go sour while being transported, so Orléans became famous for vinegar.

Vin de Pays du Jardin de la France

Wines using this denomination are produced throughout the Loire. Often they are wines made from

The cellars of the well-known merchants, Marc Brédif at Rochecorbon. Here, historic vintages of Vouvray are kept in this cellar cut into the tufa cliff, alongside the river Loire.

MONTLOUIS
**Domaine des Liards
(Berger Frères)** 70, rue de Chenonceaux, 37270 St Martin le Beau. Tel: 02 47 50 67 36. Fax: 02 47 50 21 13. Mon-Fri 0830-1200, 1400-1900, Sat, Sun by appointment only.

TOURAINE
Confrérie des Vignerons de Oisly et Thesée Le Bourg, 41700 Oisly. Tel: 02 54 79 75 20. Fax: 02 54 79 75 29.

VOUVRAY
Ets. Marc Brédif 87, Quai de la Loire, 37210 Rochecorbon. Tel: 02 47 52 50 07. Fax: 02 47 52 53 41. (M. Malbrant). Mon-Fri 0900-1200, 1330-1800. Weekends and holidays from Easter to All Saints Day. 1100-1300, 1500-1800. 10th-century rock cellars. TF.WS.E. ☎ E-mail: Bredif.loire@wanadoo.fr
Huet SA Le Haut Lieu, 37210 Vouvray. Tel: 02 47 52 78 87. Fax: 02 47 52 66 51. TF.E.

FOR FURTHER INFORMATION
C.I.V.T. 19, Square Prosper-Mérimée, 37000 Tours. Tel: 02 47 05 40 01. Fax: 02 47 66 57 32.

WINE FESTIVALS
Amboise Wine Fair Easter.
Azay end Mar
Bourgeuil 1st weekend Mar
Cravant Ascension Day
Montlouis Pentecost.
Panzoult (Chinon) 1 May
Vouvray Wine Festival early Feb.

grape varieties that are not permitted under *appellation contrôlée* rules. For instance, in most Loire appellations, pure Chardonnay is not allowed, so producers label it as *vin de pays*.

Touraine
This is the heart of the Loire valley. Here you will find many of the famous châteaux like Amboise, Azay-Le-Rideau, Chenonceau, Cheverny, Loches, Ussé (the inspiration for the Sleeping Beauty) and Villandry, as well as a host of delightful but lesser-known châteaux such as Montpoupon near Montrichard. There is a little château or manor house around almost every corner!

Although Tours is the chief city, its size means that it is not the ideal base. Instead it is far more pleasant to find a hotel in the peaceful and gentle Touraine countryside. The vineyards of Touraine stretch from the edge of the Sologne, a large area of forest and lakes, in the east to Chinon and St Nicolas de Bourgueil in the west. However the vines are by no means continuous.

Eastern Touraine is the transitional zone between the Central Vineyards and those of the rest of the Loire. There are a large number of grape varieties grown here. As well as Gamay, Pinot Noir and Sauvignon Blanc, you start to find Cabernet Franc and Chenin Blanc, which are the best and dominant varieties in the rest of Touraine as well as Anjou-Saumur. Producers here tend to make up to a dozen different wines and have all three colors.

The basic Touraine appellation covers most of these wines. They offer some of the best value in the Loire. Look out for the easy drinking, soft Gamays, crunchy Sauvignon Blancs but avoid those with a pungent vegetal reek which comes from unripe grapes, and Cabernets. In good years, the Cabernets can age remarkably well. The dark colored Côt (known elsewhere as Malbec) is also worth trying. Many of the vineyards are along the pretty Cher valley, especially between St Aignan and Bléré and also

BOURGUEIL
Maison Audebert et Fils ave Jean Causeret, 37140 Bourgueil. Tel: 02 47 97 70 06. Fax: 02 47 97 72 07. (M. Jean-Claude Audebert). Mon-Fri 0900-1200, 1330-1830. Closed Sat-Sun (except by prior appointment). Historic cellars, collection of wine implements. TF.WS.E. www.tourisme-info.com/ vignoble/audebert
Régis Mureau La Gaucherie, Ingrandes de Touraine, 37140 Bourgueil. Tel: 02 47 96 97 60. Fax: 02 47 96 93 43. TF.WS. ☎

CHINON
Christophe & Jean Baudry Domaine de la Perrière, 37500 Cravant les Coteaux. Tel: 02 47 93 15 79. Fax: 02 47 98 44 44. Mon-Fri 0900-1230, 1400-1800, Sat 0900-1330.
Maison Couly Dutheil 12, rue Diderot, B.P. 234 37502 Chinon. Tel: 02 47 97 20 20. Fax: 02 47 97 20 25. Mon-Fri 0800-1200, 1400-1800. Sat 0800-1200. Rock cellars. TF.WS.E. www.coulydutheil-chinon.com
S.C.E.A. Charles Joguet Sazilly, 37220 l'Ile Bouchard. Tel: 02 47 58 55 53. Fax: 02 47 58 52 22. (M. Alain Delaunay). Mon-Fri 0800-1200, 1400-1800. TF.WS.E. ☎ www.vinteanet.fr/charlesjoguet

WINE FESTIVALS
Bourgueil and **St-Nicolas-de-Bourgueil** Wine fair 1st weekend Mar.
Azay-le-Rideau Wine Fair last Sat in Feb.

up on the plateau between the Cher and the Loire, especially around Oisly.

Three towns or villages, Amboise, Azay-le-Rideau and Mesland, are allowed to add their names to the basic Touraine appellation. This ought to mean that these wines are superior to basic Touraine but in practice this is not necessarily the case.

Cheverny and Valençay
The imposing Château of Cheverny was built in 1634. Much more recently, the wines of Cheverny, which lie between the small eponymous town and Blois, were promoted to AC status. The reds are made from Gamay and Pinot Noir and the whites largely from Sauvignon Blanc with a little Chardonnay.

Curiously, Cour-Cheverny is a separate AC. It is reserved for whites made from Romorantin, a unique local grape variety. The resulting wine is pleasant enough but the fact that no-one has ever bothered to plant Romorantin elsewhere is a fair indicator of its potential.

Valençay's greatest claim to fame is that its château was the home of Talleyrand – one of the most flexible of politicians – who served in government before, during and after the French Revolution without losing his head. Valençay's VDQS wines are of local interest.

Vouvray and Montlouis
Close to Tours are the twin appellations of Vouvray and Montlouis, which face each other across the Loire with the better-known Vouvray on the north bank and the smaller appellation of Montlouis on the south. The sole variety here is Chenin Blanc, the great white grape of the Loire.

Chenin is a remarkable variety as it can be used to make still or sparkling wine. The still wines can range from bone dry to lusciously sweet. (In South Africa, Chenin is even used to make fortified wines and brandy.) The grape's relatively high acidity means that these wines have a great potential to age: well made wines from even moderate vintages can easily last for fifty years or more.

Driving through the center of Montlouis and Vouvray, you will see no sign of vines, although there are signs offering wines for sale. Instead, the vines are grown along the top of the slopes overlooking the Loire and on the plateau.
Many growers have their cellars dug into the limestone hillsides. There are also troglodyte (cave dweller) houses. The vineyards of Vouvray run from Rochecorbon in the west along to Vouvray, where they turn up the valley of the Brenne to Vernou and Chançay. The best wines tend to come from the south-facing vineyards of Rochecorbon and Vouvray. Across the river most of the Montlouis vineyards lie to the east of the town of Montlouis, between the Loire and the small town of Saint Martin-le-Beau in the Cher valley. The appellation of Montlouis is a sixth of the size of its neighbor.

The wines of Vouvray and Montlouis are broadly similar. Depending on the year, they can cover the full range from dry white to sweet, still and sparkling.

Jasnières and the Loir Valley
Some 40 km (25 miles) north of the Loire is the valley of Le Loir. The Loir is a tributary of the Loire. It flows parallel to the Loire until it joins up with the Sarthe and the

Mayenne to become the Maine, and joins the Loire just to the west of Angers. The Loir is a very pretty, pastoral valley with a few areas of vines. Jasnières, near to the attractive little town of La Chartre-sur-Loir, is the best known. With slopes facing due south, this is again pure Chenin Blanc territory.

The wines are generally dry but some demi-sec and sweet (*moelleux*) wines are made in good years.

Surrounding Jasnières is the AC Coteaux du Loir. Here whites are made from Chenin and reds from Gamay and Pinot d'Aunis, a peppery local variety. Also in the valley are the VDQS Coteaux du Vendômois, which are made in all three colors from a number of varieties. While in the Loir, it is worth visiting Vendôme for its remarkable gothic cathedral; Lavardin for its ruined fortress and very old church, which is tiny and has

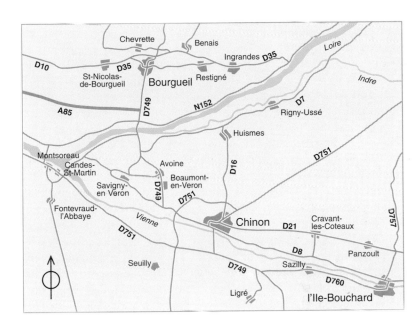

The 16th-century Château of Azay-le-Rideau is one of the most beautiful along the length of the Loire. It has a wonderful collection of antique furniture and tapestries. In the neighborhood are made crisp white and rosé wines, whose success is restricted only by the very limited quantities that are made.

some equally old murals; the little market town of Montoire; and Trôo with its many troglodyte houses.

Chinon and Bourgueil

West of Tours there are few vineyards, apart from the little enclave around Azay-le-Rideau, until you reach the red wine appellations of Chinon and Bourgueil at the western end of Touraine. This is the start of the Kingdom of Cabernet Franc.

In Bordeaux, apart from the wines of Cheval Blanc, Cabernet Franc has a minor role compared to its cousin Cabernet Sauvignon. But it is the other way round in the Loire. Cabernet Franc is undoubtedly the best red of the valley, while in most years Cabernet Sauvignon struggles to ripen properly. Chinon is the best place to start a tour of this area. Approach the town from the south which gives you a magnificent view of the ruined château and the river Vienne with the medieval town squeezed between the two.

Apart from a small amount of white Chinon made from Chenin Blanc, these wines are essentially red, although a small amount of rosé is also made. The wines from Chinon are softer and more approachable than those from Bourgueil and St Nicolas, which tend to be more tannic and need time in bottle to soften up. Chinon also has the great advantage of being easy to pronounce. The town is associated with Rabelais, who was born nearby at La Divinière close to the village of Seuilly.

There are three types of soil in the area giving three different types of wine. Around the confluence of the Vienne and Loire, the soil is sandy and the wines are light and often bottled early for drinking in the

Spring following the vintage. Gravel beds are widespread in all three appellations, especially in St Nicolas de Bourgueil.

The wines from the *graviers* are more full bodied and need a little more time before they are ready to drink. However, it is the wines that come from grapes grown on the limestone *coteaux* that are the most full bodied and the most long lived.

You would be very hard put to it to distinguish between a Bourgueil and St-Nicolas-de Bourgueil. Its existence as a separate appellation is normally ascribed to St-Nicolas having had a forceful mayor when the appellation was created in 1937. He insisted that his village deserved its own appellation and must not be swallowed up by its larger neighbor Bourgueil three miles away.

Anjou-Saumur

The vineyards of Saumur start just beyond Candes St Martin where the Vienne joins the Loire. The main road along the south bank to Saumur

SAUMUR
Caves des Vignerons de Saumur 49260 St Cyr-en-Bourg. Tel: 02 41 53 06 06. Fax: 02 41 53 06 10. Every day 0930-1830. T.F.E.

Régis Neau Domaine de Nerleux, 4 Rue de la Paleine, 49260 St Cyr-en-Bourg. Tel: 02 41 51 61 04: Fax: 02 41 51 65 34. Mon-Fri 1800-1200, 1400-1800, Sat 0800-1200. T.F.E.

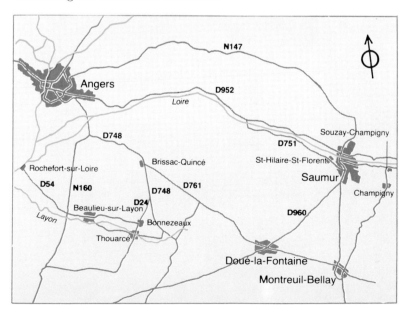

passes through the small villages of Parnay and Souzay-Champigny. Just as at Vouvray, there are no signs of vines from the main road: the vineyards lie on the slopes above the old river cliffs.

Saumur Champigny

These are the vineyards of Saumur-Champigny, one of the best reds of the Loire. Depending on the *cuvée* and the ambitions of the grower, they range in style from young, light summer quaffers to serious reds which need to be aged to show their best. Outside the Saumur-Champigny zone, the reds are plain AC Saumur. They tend to be good value, early

drinking wines. Many of the best come from further south from the area around Le Puy-Notre-Dame.

Whites are mainly made from Chenin Blanc. The overall quality has improved greatly over the past ten years. Dry whites have the AC Saumur Blanc, while the local sweet wines are called AC Coteaux de Saumur.

Cave des Vignerons de St Cyr

One of the best-run co-operatives in France is on the outskirts of the small town of St Cyr, a few miles south of Saumur. There is an enormous cellar under the winery, which is big enough to take trucks.

The capital of Anjou is the city of Angers, known not just for its wines, but also for Cointreau liqueur. Dominating the town is the magnificent medieval castle.

SAUMUR (cont)
Bouvet Ladubay rue de l'Abbaye, St-Hilaire-St Florent, 49400 Saumur. Tel: 02 41 83 83 83. Fax: 02 41 50 24 32. (Jean-Maurice Belayche or Véronique Bocot). Every day 1000-1200, 1430-1800. Sparkling wines, audio-visual presentation, rock cellars, contemporary art center. Tutored tastings by prior appointment. TF.WS.E.

The red wines of Saumur-Champigny, made mainly from the Cabernet Franc grape, are now amongst the most fashionable in France, largely due to their refreshing fruitiness. Here is a typical tasting cellar.

ANGERS
Maison du Vin de l'Anjou 5 bis, Place Kennedy, 49100 Angers. Tel: 02 41 88 81 13. Fax: 02 41 86 71 84. Tue-Sun 0900-1300, 1400-1830.

ANJOU AND BONNEZEAUX
SCEA Daviau Domaine de Bablut, 49320 Brissac-Quince. Tel: 02 41 91 22 59. Fax: 02 41 91 24 77. Mon-Sat 0900-1200, 1400-1830. T.F.E.

Château de Fesles Vignobles Germain & Associes, 49380 Thouarcé. Tel: 02 41 68 94 00. Fax: 02 41 68 94 01. One of the leading properties in Anjou. Recently restored. T.F.E.

Sparkling Saumur
Saumur is the center of the production of Loire sparkling wine. Ackerman-Laurance is the oldest house. The company was established in 1811. Because of the limestone soil, the local wines have a natural tendency to sparkle and the limestone hillsides are ideally suited for constructing extensive cellars where the bottles can be stacked up to mature. Chenin Blanc is the chief variety along with Chardonnay and Cabernet Franc.

Most of the big Saumur houses have their premises in St Hilaire-St-Florent, just to the west of Saumur. The exception is Gratien & Meyer, which is to the east of the town.

As well as Saumur Mousseux, sparkling wines from Vouvray and Montlouis are well worth trying. In particular, look out for Vouvray or Montlouis Pétillant. This local specialty is a more delicate sparkler as it has less pressure (2.5 atmospheres) than the more customary five atmospheres used in Champagne and other sparkling wines. In theory at least, Crémant de Loire is a higher

quality sparkling wine with stricter regulations, based on those used in Champagne. It can come from anywhere in Anjou-Saumur and Touraine.

Anjou
In Anjou the soil changes from the limestone and clay of the Paris basin to the hard, impervious rocks of the Brittany peninsula. This is an area of granite, schist and slate. This change also affects the wines. The whites tend to be softer because they have less acidity and the reds are often more tannic.

Most of the Anjou vineyards are south of the Loire, around the valleys of the Layon and the much smaller Aubance. Rosé, especially Rosé d'Anjou, remains by volume the most important wine made. But this semi-sweet wine is far from the most interesting.

Coteaux du Layon and Coteaux de l'Aubance
The longest-lived and most fascinating wines of Anjou are the sweet wines from these two valleys. At their best they are among the great sweet wines of the world. They have to be made from Chenin Blanc. Although these wines can be very rich, they also have Chenin's acidity to balance them and stop them being cloying.

The ideal conditions for making sweet wines are warm fall days that start with misty mornings. These conditions produce noble rot or botrytis. Although this type of rot makes the outside of the grape look disgusting, it eats up the water content of the grape and so concentrates its sugars. Growers wait until the grapes are affected by botrytis and then pick selectively.

Typically a vineyard will be picked over three or four times, taking only those bunches affected by botrytis.

Bonnezeaux and Quarts de Chaume

These are two small Grand Cru appellations in the Layon valley. They are two particularly favored sites and have special micro-climates which are very prone to autumnal noble rot. The showpiece of Bonnezeaux is Château de Fesles, which has a dominant position overlooking the Bonnezeaux vineyard. It is now owned by Bernard Germain, a Bordeaux producer. He bought the property in late 1995 and is making some exceptional wines.

Quarts de Chaume is further west. The vineyards are in an amphitheater facing due south. At their best,

The leaves change color in the Coulée du Serrant vineyard of Savennières. Here are made some of the greatest dry white wines of the Loire vineyards.

Quarts de Chaume have great concentration as well as delicacy. These wines will keep for at least fifty years even in moderate vintages.

Savennières

This is the third Grand Cru of Anjou. Once again the grape is Chenin Blanc, but the wines are dry, although in very hot years they may be *demi-sec*. The vineyards are on the north bank of the Loire just a few miles west of Angers.

Savennières is a very minerally flavored wine and, although it can be enjoyed young, it needs five or ten years to show its best. It is the ideal partner for a classic Loire poached

WINE FESTIVALS
Fête de la Vigne et du vin Held in various parts of Anjou-Saumur, weekend of Ascension
Angers *Salon des Vins de Loire* 1st Mon, Tue and Wed of Feb.
Brissac *Concours des Anjou Villages* last weekend Nov
Saumur Wine Fair 2nd weekend Feb.
St Lambert du Lattay early July
St Aubin mid July

FOR FURTHER INFORMATION
C.I.V.A.S. Hôtel des Vins, 73, rue Plantagenet, 49100 Angers. Tel: 02 41 87 62 57. Fax: 02 41 86 71 84. www.vins-valdeloire.com

ANCENIS
Les Vignerons de la Noelle
44150 Ancenis. Tel:
02 40 98 92 72. Fax:
02 40 98 96 70. Mon 1400-
1800; Tue-Fri 0900-1200,
1400-1800; Sat 0900-1200.
Wines from Anjou, Ancenis
and Muscadet. TF.WS.E.G.
E-mail: vavenel@cana.fr

LA CHAPELLE-HEULIN
Donatien-Bahuaud 44330
La Chapelle-Heulin. Tel:
02 40 06 70 05. Fax: 02 40
06 77 11. (Marie-France
Cormerais). Mon-Fri 0900-
1200, 1400-1700. TF.WS.E.

LE LANDREAU
Domaines Luneau-Papin
Domaine Pierre de la
Grange, 44430 Le Landreau.
Tel: 02 40 06 45 27.
Fax: 02 40 06 46.62. TF.

fish served with *beurre blanc*. There
are a number of châteaux and large
manor houses in the country around
Savennières. Many of these imposing
edifices were built by merchants from
Angers.

Anjou Rouge and Anjou Blanc
As well as making Anjou Villages,
most producers also make an easy-
drinking Anjou Rouge. This wine is
designed to be light and to be ready
as soon as it is put on the market,
usually in the Spring following the
vintage.

In high summer, Anjou Rouge is
often served lightly chilled. Anjou
Blanc can be dry or demi-sec and
a blend of Chenin with 20%
Chardonnay. Increasingly, the best
growers are using only 100% Chenin
Blanc in their product.

Anjou Villages
As the popularity of rosés declined in
the late 1970s and early 1980s,
vignerons increasingly turned to
making red wines. In 1985 the AC
Anjou Villages was created. This is
for red only. Cabernet Franc and
Cabernet Sauvignon are the
permitted varieties. Anjou Villages
cannot go on sale until the
September following the vintage.
These wines are generally best after
three to five years.

Muscadet
Muscadet is one of the great
matches with fish and, in particular,
shellfish. Fortunately for the visitor,
Nantes is close to the sea, so there
are plenty of *plateaux fruits de mers*
available to wash down with a chilled
bottle of Muscadet.

*Originally from Burgundy, the Melon grape has
now taken the name of the wine it produces, the
Muscadet. Here in the late spring, the vineyards
turn into seas of green.*

The Sèvre-et-Maine is one of the most intensely planted vineyards of France. Much of the vineyard is quite flat, with short, steep slopes down into the valleys of the Sèvre and Maine and their tributaries.

In terms of volume, this is the most important vine-growing area of the Loire. Much of the wine is white. There are three areas around Nantes. The Sèvre et Maine is reckoned to make the best Muscadet, but growers from Muscadet Coteaux de la Loire and the Côtes de Grandlieu probably would not agree. Muscadet Coteaux de Loire comes from around the town of Ancenis, east of Nantes and on the north bank of the Loire, while the Côtes de Grandlieu comes from vineyards around the lake of the same name.

Muscadet is made from the Melon de Bourgogne, which as its name suggests originally came from Burgundy. As the Melon does not

The town of Ancenis lies on the north bank of the river Loire, between the vineyards of Muscadet and Anjou. The Co-operative cellar is located close to the Château.

have a strong personality, the wine needs some contact with the lees to give it added yeasty flavor. Look out for the words *sur lie* on the bottle. This means that the wine was bottled straight off the fine lees. A *sur lie* should have a slight prickle of carbon dioxide at the back of the throat when you swallow.

Even drier than Muscadet is the lemony Gros Plant. Poor versions can be unbearably and unbelievably acid but good ones make your mouth water and think of a dozen succulent oysters.

Gros Plant was originally planted in the area by the Dutch to turn into brandy, which is why it is also planted in Cognac. Like Muscadet look out for a *sur lie*, which will put a little flesh onto the thin bones of Gros Plant. It is also used as a base for sparkling wine.

ST FIACRE SUR MAINE
Château de Chasseloir
44690 St Fiacre sur Maine. Tel: 02 40 54 81 15. Fax: 02 40 54 81 70. (M. Bernard Chereau Jr.) Every day 0800-1800. 18th-century tower, historic cellars. TF.WS.E ☎
Louis Métaireau La Févrie, près St Fiacre, 44690 Maison-sur-Sèvre. Tel: 02 40 54 81 92. Fax: 02 40 54 87 83. (Mme Marie-Luce Métaireau). Mon-Fri 0800-1200,1400-1800. TF.WS.E. (☎ evenings and weekends.)

HAUTE-GOULAINE
Marquis de Goulaine
Château de Goulaine, 44115 Haute-Goulaine. Tel: 02 40 54 91 42. Fax: 02 40 54 90 23. 1 Apr-15 Jun, 16 Sep-1 Nov, Sat, Sun, holidays only, 1400-1800. 16 Jun-15 Sep, Wed-Mon 1400-1800 (closed Tue). Historic château, tropical butterflies. TP.WS.E.G.S.

VALLET
Château des Rois 12, rue des Rois, 44330 Vallet. Tel: 02 40 33 99 94. Fax: 02 40 36 26 53. (Delphine Méchineau or Magali Cesbron). Mon-Fri 0800-1200, 1400-1700. TF.WS.E.G. ☎ E-mail: michel.bahuaud@wanadoo.fr
Sauvion et Fils Château de Cléray, 44330 Vallet. Tel: 02 40 36 22 55. Fax: 02 40 36 34 62. (Brigitte Brunetière). Easter-end Sep, Mon-Fri 0900-1200, 1400-1700, otherwise by appointment. TF.E. ☎ E-mail: sauvion44@aol.com

WINE MUSEUM
Musée du Vignoble Nantais
82, rue Pierre Abélard, 44330 Le Pallet. Tel: 02 40 80 90 13. Fax: 02 40 80 49 81. 15 Mar-15 Nov, every day.

Cognac

Cognac is one of the greatest spirits in the world. It is a brandy, the distillation of wine, and as there are many whiskies, so are there many brandies, but only two of them, Cognac and Armagnac, have reputations based firmly on the source of their wines and the method of distillation.

The fertile chalky countryside around the town of Cognac, on the river Charente, gives thin, acid wines with a low alcoholic degree. It is such wines that give the finest brandies, and since distillation began in the region at the beginning of the 15th century, it has built up for itself a proud reputation for quality. The nature of the product lends itself to brand promotion and there are a few companies that dominate world markets. They may not, however, actually own vineyards, or even distil the Cognacs they sell, so there is a broad range of places for the interested tourist to visit.

There are four basic factors that go into the production of a Cognac: the soil, the grapes, the distillation and the ageing.

The area within which Cognac may be produced is quite large, most of the two *départements* of the Charentes. There are vineyards on the Ile de Ré and the Ile d'Oléron in the Atlantic; on the north bank of the Gironde estuary; and around the three towns in the heart of the region, Cognac itself, Jarnac and Saintes. In each of these areas, different soils produce different qualities of wine, giving different qualities of spirit.

For example, a Cognac from the sandy soil of the Ile de Ré may even have a hint of iodine in its flavor from its proximity to the sea. A Cognac from the chalky soil to the south of Cognac itself will have the most finesse and bouquet.

Because of these factors, there is an elaborate hierarchy within the vineyard areas, and the price of the resultant spirit will vary considerably.

The finest region is the Grande Champagne to the south of Cognac, then the Petite Champagne, and through the Borderies, Fins Bois, Bons Bois and the fringe Bois Ordinaires and Bois à Terroir.

You can find a Cognac labeled Grande Champagne, which means that it has been distilled solely from wines from that region. A Fine Champagne will be a blend of Grande and Petite Champagne. Most Cognacs, however, will be a blend created to a standard by the various companies from several regions.

Cognac production

The grape varieties grown are mainly the Saint-Emilion, the Colombard and the Folle Blanche, which are often picked before they are fully ripe to ensure sufficient acidity.

During the winter, as soon as the wine has finished fermenting, distillation takes place in a copper pot still, fired by a naked flame. Double distillation ensures that the spirit is as pure as possible.

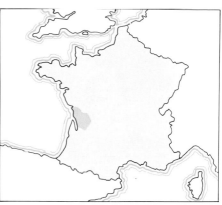

To get to Cognac
Cognac is 476km (297 miles) from Paris and 242km (151 miles) from Tours by the A10, D939, N150 and D731.

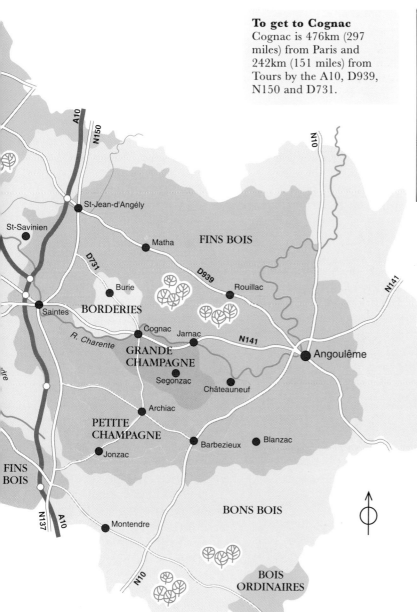

COGNAC
Les Quais Hennessy
Quai Richard Hennessy, 16100 Cognac. Tel: 05 45 35 72 68. Fax: 05 45 35 79 49. Every day 1 Mar-31 Dec (closed 1 May, 25 Dec). Jun-Sep 1000-1800; 12 Mar-May, Oct-Dec 1000-1700. Guided tour in 5 languages. TF (with entry charge. Group concessions.) WS.E.G.N.S. www.hennessy-cognac.com

Martell & Co. place Edouard Martell, 16100 Cognac. Tel: 05 45 36 33 33. Fax: 05 45 36 33 39. (Mrs Ricard). Jul, Aug Mon-Fri 0945-1700. Sat, Sun 1000-1615. Jun, Sept Mon-Fri 0930-1100, 1200-1700; Oct-May Mon-Thu visits at 0930, 1100, 1430, 1545, 1700, closed holidays. Free guided tour with presentation. Shop. TF.WS.E. E-mail: caroline-ricard@ seagram.com

Cognac Otard S.A. Château de Cognac, 16101 Cognac. Tel: 05 45 36 88 86. Fax: 05 45 36 88 89. Apr-Oct, every day (except 1 May); Nov-Dec, every day except Sat, Sun and holidays. Jan-Mar, open for goups on request. Guided tour (45 mins) at 1000, 1100, 1400, 1500, 1600 and 1700. Audio-visual presentation. Historic château. TF (with entry charge). WS.E.G.I.S.

COGNAC (cont.)
Philippe Naud le Buisson, St Laurent de Cognac, 16100 Cognac. Tel: 05 45 82 74 70. Fax: 05 45 36 19 01. Every day 0800-1200, 1400-1800. Also wine, chocolates. TF.WS.

JARNAC
Courvoisier S.A 16200 Jarnac. Tel: 05 45 35 56 16 (Museum). Fax: 05 45 35 55 00. Free guided tours daily. Jun-Sep 0930-1800, Oct-May 0930-1100, 1400-1800; last visit 1700. Napoleonic and Cognac museum, audio-visual presentation and cellars. Free miniature. WS.E.G.N.S.

ST-JEAN-D'ANGELY
Cognac Louis Bouron S.A La Grange, 17416 St-Jean-d'Angély. Tel: 05 46 32 00 12. Fax: 05 46 32 06 11. (Mme Parias). Every day 0900-1900. 15th-century château. TF.WS.E.G.S. E-mail: cognaclouisbouron@ swfrance.com www.swfrance.com/ louisbouron.htm

"The angels' share"
The new spirit is harsh and fiery, so it is put to age in casks of local, Tronçais or Limousin oak. The length of time that it is allowed to age depends on the individual company. During this time the spirit mellows and softens: there is heavy evaporation – I have seen one estimate of the equivalent of 20 million bottles each year. This evaporation, locally called "the angels' share," blackens the roofs of the warehouses and gives a grimy, industrial air to many of the buildings of Cognac.

Cognac labels
On Cognac labels, there can be a bewildering variety of quality symbols such as the familiar three star symbol, VSOP (Very Superior Old Pale) and Napoléon. Age controls in Cognac extend only as far as $6^1/_2$ years in barrel. Thirty months is the minimum aging period. Cognacs of less than $4^1/_2$ years can only be labelled *** or VS. The youngest spirit in a VSOP, VO or Réserve must be $4^1/_2$ years old, and for Napoléon, XO, Extra, Hors d'Age it must be $6^1/_2$ years. In many cases the bulk of the Cognac may be considerably older.

Most companies will have small stocks of exceptionally old cognacs, which they store in a warehouse called "paradise." This spirit may no longer be stored in casks, but in glass carboys.

Pineau des Charentes
There is one other local specialty that should be tasted. This is the *Pineau des Charentes*, which comes in two forms, white and rosé. *Pineau* is a fortified drink made by mixing sweet, unfermented grape juice with one-year-old brandy, and then leaving them to marry for 18 months or more in oak barrels.

Scenery and historic towns
The Cognac region is pleasant and varied. It is not a region of intensive viticulture: it is just as renowned, though perhaps in different circles, for its dairy products.

There are beautiful beaches at Royan and on the Ile d'Oléron. You can hire a boat on the languid river Charente: until recently the brandy-boats used to come up it to the little port of Tonnay-Charente to load.

There are also a number of beautiful historic towns. In Cognac, the 10th-century castle now belongs to the Otard company, but it was in the hands of the English for many years, after Richard the Lionheart married his bastard son Philip to Amélie of Cognac. Later the castle was rebuilt by Guy de Lusignan, the son of the widow of King John.

Like many of the other important companies in the region, Otard was

Vines from three different ages in Cognac. Top left, those that have just been planted; in the middle, some that have been planted a year ago; and mature vines, which will give the acid wine that makes the best spirit.

founded by a British family: the Martells were from the Channel Islands; the Hines from Dorset; and the Hennessys and the Exshaws from Ireland.

Saintes

Historically, the capital of the region was Saintes, some 26km (16 miles) to the west. This was an important Roman town and there are still a number of remains, including an amphitheater and a triumphal arch. While not a great deal of the former remains, you can still see where the wild beasts were caged.

The arch originally stood on the Roman bridge over the Charente. It was erected during the reign of Nero by Caius Julius Rufus to the memory of Germanicus, Tiberius and Drusus.

In 1844, it was dismantled and re-erected where it now stands.

Just off the N137, which leads north-west out of Saintes, is the beautiful Château de la Roche-Courbon, near Saint-Porchaire. Jonzac, too, has a very fine 15th-century castle.

La Rochelle

In the north-west corner of the Cognac region, the pretty port of La Rochelle should be visited. Here the inner harbour is protected by the twin towers of La Chaîne and Saint-Nicolas. Finally, in the extreme east of the area is the important town of Angoulême, with its impressive girdle of fortifications.

In Cognac, the spirit is distilled twice in these traditional "pot" stills.

ST MEME LES CARRIERES
Cognac Ménard
16720 St Même les Carrières. Tel: 05 45 81 90 26. Fax: 05 45 81 98 22. Mon-Fri 0800-1200, 1400-1800. Cellar visit. TF.WS.E. www.cognac-menard.com

FOR FURTHER INFORMATION
Cognac
B.N.I.C. 23, allées du Champ de Mars, 16101 Cognac. Tel: 05 45 35 60 00. Fax: 05 45 82 86 54. E.G.I.S. E-mail: comm@bnic.fr
Pineau des Charentes
Comité National du Pineau des Charentes
112, ave Victor Hugo, 16100 Cognac. Tel: 05 45 32 09 27. Fax: 05 45 35 42 25. Mon-Fri 0900-1200, 1400-1800. TF.E.I.S.

Bordeaux

Representatives of the various confréries, *or drinking brotherhoods, of Bordeaux. Each region has its own association, with its individual robes and ceremonies.*

There are many reasons why the favorite French wines among English-speaking people have traditionally been those from Bordeaux. First of all, the province of Aquitaine belonged to the English Crown for more than three hundred years.

Secondly, the situation of Bordeaux as a port has made it ideal for the shipment of wine to Britain and the United States. Even during the German occupation in World War II, the gesture that the local resistance fighters made in order to secure more arms from Britain was to load a few casks of their best wine on to a boat and sail for England. Another reason can be seen in the names within the trade. Among the merchants there are Lawtons and Bartons, and the vineyard names include such as Cantenac-Brown, Clarke and Boyd. These are good historical reasons for our interest.

The vineyards of Bordeaux cover a vast area along both banks of the Gironde, and of the two rivers whose estuary this is: the Dordogne and the Garonne. Within this area is a broad range of styles of wine, ranging from the classic red wines of the Haut-Médoc, based on the Cabernet Sauvignon grape, and of St.-Emilion, on the Merlot, to the dry white wines of the Graves and the luscious sweet wines of Sauternes. However, the great wines with famous names form only a minute proportion of the total production. It has been claimed that there are over three thousand château names in Bordeaux, but of these only a handful are known to even the most devoted wine lover.

The meaning of *château*
It must be pointed out that in Bordeaux the word "château" may be used in one of its two generally accepted senses – a castle or an imposing country house. However, here the word may also be used to mean anything from the most impressive of palaces to a country cottage, or even a barn. There may not even be a building. The word has come to be synonymous with a vineyard, and not necessarily a distinct vineyard at that, for now many properties sell their second wine under a separate château name. Bordeaux, then, is not just Margaux, Yquem and Cheval Blanc. They may be the apex of the pyramid, but there is a solid base of lesser wines that probably never appear under individual vineyard names.

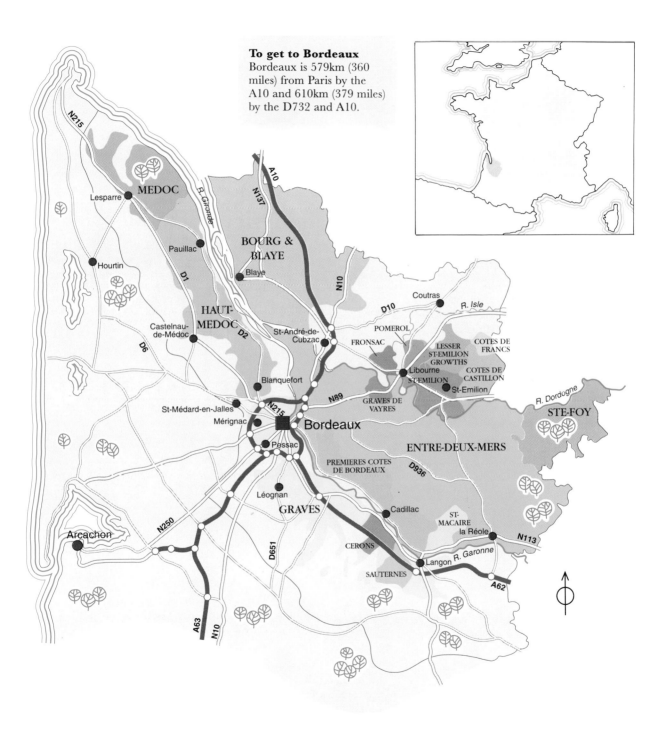

To get to Bordeaux
Bordeaux is 579km (360 miles) from Paris by the A10 and 610km (379 miles) by the D732 and A10.

N215

A10

N137

MEDOC

Lesparre

R. Gironde

Pauillac

Hourtin

BOURG & BLAYE

Blaye

N10

D1

HAUT-MEDOC

Castelnau-de-Médoc

D2

St-André-de-Cubzac

D6

Blanquefort

St-Médard-en-Jalles

N215

N89

Mérignac

Bordeaux

Pessac

Léognan

Arcachon

N250

GRAVES

D651

Léognan

Cadillac

CERONS

SAUTERNES

A63
N10

D10

Coutras

R. Isle

POMEROL

FRONSAC

LESSER ST-EMILION GROWTHS

COTES DE FRANCS

Libourne
ST-EMILION

COTES DE CASTILLON

St-Emilion

R. Dordogne

STE-FOY

GRAVES DE VAYRES

ENTRE-DEUX-MERS

D936

PREMIERES COTES DE BORDEAUX

ST-MACAIRE
la Réole

N113

Langon R. Garonne

A62

The City of Bordeaux

Coming into Bordeaux from the north, across the Pont de Pierre, the city unfolds in a vast semi-circle to the right, presenting one of the most attractive waterfronts anywhere in the world. Many of the finest buildings, surrounding the Place de la Bourse, were built in the middle of the 18th century. Further to the right is the Esplanade des Quinconces and further still, the Quai des Chartrons, the former center of the Bordeaux wine trade. Just behind all these are such wonderful buildings as the Grand Theater and the narrow streets of the old city.

On these quays, from which ships sailed all over the world, the wealthy merchants had their warehouses, With the coming of long-distance lorries and container-ports, little wine now leaves Bordeaux by boat. However, the *quais* continue to be used by cruise ships, carrying mainly passengers from the U.S.A.

The warehouses

Most of the merchants have moved to purpose-built, temperature-controlled warehouses outside the city. Only a few retain their token presence on the Chartrons. In their day, these warehouses, too, were custom-built, running back in narrow strips for a quarter of a mile or more behind the offices at the front. They were cool, for their walls were thick and the barrels could be rolled along the narrow railways provided. The office boy would often ride from one end of the cellar to the other on a bicycle.

There are a few remains from the time when Bordeaux was a Roman city, but among other monuments, the Tour du Prince Noir (the Tower of the Black Prince) bears witness to the time of English occupation.

The waterfront at Bordeaux, which has been described as the most splendid in Europe. Today, fewer boats moor against the historic quays, but Bordeaux is still a thriving city.

Graves

The vineyards of Graves come right to the door of Bordeaux. Many have disappeared in the face of rising land prices, but there are still four notable vineyards, even within the motorway corset that now restricts Bordeaux on the southern side.

Of these the most famous is Château Haut-Brion, which can be reached by taking the N250 road in the direction of Arcachon, from the center of the city. Haut-Brion was classified in 1855 as a *premier grand cru*; the only vineyard from outside the Haut-Médoc to be so honored.

PESSAC
Château Pape-Clément
216, ave du Dr Nancel Pénard, 33600 Pessac.
Tel: 05 57 26 38 38.
Fax: 05 57 26 38 39.
(Eric Larramona). Mon-Fri 0900-1200, 1400-1700.
Cellars. T.F.E.S. ☎

In 1787, Thomas Jefferson tried to buy a hogshead of the famous 1784 vintage, through the local honorary American consul, but was refused. He ultimately managed to buy a few cases of "Obrion," which he shared with a friend.

In 1934, the then owner offered the vineyard to the city of Bordeaux, but the gesture was rejected and it was bought by the American banking family, the Dillons, in whose hands it has since remained.

The other châteaux close to the city are La Mission Haut-Brion, La Tour Haut-Brion and, in neighboring Pessac, Pape-Clément. All these vineyards are particularly known for their red wines, and this is true of all the vineyards of that northern part of the Graves, closest to Bordeaux.

A new appellation, Pessac Léognan, was created in 1987.

Léognan

For the amateur with just a little time to spend in Bordeaux, Léognan on the D651 may be the place to visit. Here are such well-known châteaux as Olivier, Haut-Bailly and Domaine de Chevalier.

LEOGNAN
Château Carbonnieux
33850 Léognan. Tel: 05 57 96 56 20. Fax: 05 57 96 59 19. Mon-Fri 0800-1200, 1400-1800. T.P.E.G.S. ☎
Domain de Chevalier
33850 Léognan. Tel: 05 56 64 16 16. Fax: 05 56 64 18 18. (M. Bernard). Mon-Fri 0900-1200, 1400-1700. T.F.E. ☎

FOR FURTHER INFORMATION
C.I.V.B. 3, cours du XXX Juillet, 33000 Bordeaux. Tel: 05 56 00 22 66. Fax: 05 56 00 22 82. List of all châteaux welcoming visitors. G.N.S. E-mail: civbevins-bordeaux.fr

The Haut-Médoc

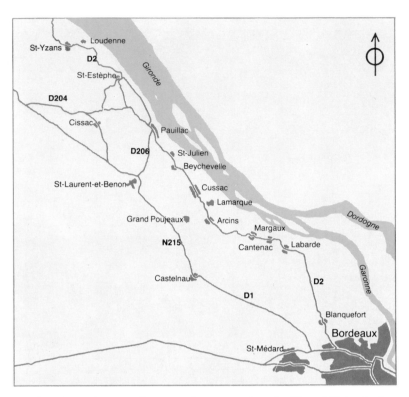

VISITING THE MEDOC

The Médoc is a long narrow vineyard, and it is difficult to do justice to the whole region in one, or even two days. As a result, if you have not been invited to stay in a château itself (and I never have), you have a choice of returning to Bordeaux each evening or finding more rural accommodation.

At one time, good hotels and restaurants in the Médoc were rare, but things have changed for the better and top-quality accommodation and food are both now available.

I suppose that the Haut-Médoc is the image of Bordeaux that most of us have in mind: noble châteaux fronted by broad sweeps of gravel and then the vines. It is the most famous region because it is from here that the best wines come – not always the most expensive, for Pétrus in Pomerol seems to have had that distinction – but the best red wines.

Alternative routes

There are two roads through the Médoc. One is the D2, which winds through the succession of wine villages and seems designed to drop you almost at the front door of every château. The other is a peculiar, but much faster, road, which starts life as the N215, becomes the D1 and then turns back into the N215 once again. This passes to the west of the vineyards, but there are a series of connecting cross-roads to the D2 so you can drive as far as

you want up the one and then return by the other. On all these roads, each individual château is clearly signposted, so you have the opportunity of making several unscheduled visits.

My recommendation is that you take the D2, which means leaving Bordeaux by the N215 and turning right on the outskirts of the city. The boundary between the Graves and the Haut-Médoc is crossed almost immediately, with the stream called the Jalle de Blanquefort.

The first classified growth, Château La Lagune, comes on the right-hand side and this is shortly followed on the left by another, Château Cantemerle.

One thing to note is that the château may not be next to its vineyards: these may be spread out in several blocks in the neighborhood.

Normally, beside the imposing château, there will also be the *chais*, or barrel-cellars. The word "cellar" is misleading, however, as with the single exception of Château Margaux, the *chais* are built above ground. Many châteaux, too, have much of their estate in meadows, woodland or garden. You can be certain, though, that if the land is capable of giving good wine, it will be planted with vines.

Margaux

With the hamlets of Labarde and Cantenac, you arrive in the area entitled to call itself Margaux, and it is here that the châteaux begin to come thick and fast. Between the two hamlets, you also cross the railway line that leads all the way up the Médoc from Bordeaux to Pointe de Grave, from where there is a ferry across the Gironde to Royan.

The current Château Margaux was built in a classical style at the beginning of the last century. On the

The elegant classical façade of Château Margaux reflects its wines' first growth status.

MARGAUX

Château d'Angludet
33460 Cantenac. Tel:
05 57 88 71 41. Fax:
05 57 88 72 52. (Sichel
family). Mon-Fri 1000-
1200, 1400-1700. T.F.E. ☎

Château Lascombes
33460 Margaux. Tel:
05 57 88 70 66. Fax:
05 57 88 72 17. (Bruno
Lemoine). Every day in
summer 1000-1730. Closed
1st. weekend each month,
Oct-Easter. TF.WS.E. ☎

Château Margaux
33460 Margaux. Tel:
05 57 88 83 83. Fax:
05 57 88 31 32. By
appointment only. Closed
Sat, Sun, Aug and during
vintage. E. ☎
www.chateau-margaux.com

**Château Prieuré-
Lichine** 33460 Cantenac.
Tel: 05 57 88 36 28.
Fax: 05 57 88 78 93.
Every day 0900-1800.
Closed 25 Dec-1 Jan.
Collection of firebacks. TF
(TP for groups). WS.E.S. ☎
E-mail: prieure.lichine@
wanadoo.fr

MOULIS EN MEDOC

Château Chasse-Spleen
Moulis en Médoc, 33480
Castelnau en Médoc. Tel:
05 56 58 02 37. Fax: 05 57
88 84 40. Mon-Fri 0900-
1230, 1400-1730. Cellars.
TF.E.G. ☎
www.chasse-spleen.com

LAMARQUE

**Ste. Civile Gromand
d'Evry** Château de
Lamarque, 33460 Lamarque.
Tel: 05 56 58 90 03 or
05 56 58 97 55. Fax:
05 56 58 93 43. Mon-Fri
0900-1200, 1400-1730. Old
fortress. Cellar visit. WS.
E-mail: chdelamarq@aol.com

same site there had been a fortress, where Edward III of England had lived. The wines of Château Margaux were classified as a first growth in 1855. They went through a bad period between 1970 and 1976, but since then they have once again climbed back into the first rank.

Château Palmer

Among the other well-known vineyards with the Margaux *appellation* is the attractive Château Palmer, which stands just on the right of the road as you go north. Officially only classified as a third growth, the reputation and price of its wines are much higher.

After the cluster of classified growths at Margaux, there is something of a lull on the D2. At Arcins, there is an important co-operative cellar for wines from the Haut-Médoc and one can turn left to see the group of châteaux, with the *appellation* of Moulis, around the village of Grand Poujeaux.

Back on the D2, you come to the village of Lamarque. Parts of its château date back to the 11th century, though most of the present structure is from the 14th. To continue the royal English tradition, it was occupied by Henry V.

Beyond Cussac, the most concentrated group of fine vineyards in the world begins at Beychevelle.

Château Beychevelle

This château used to belong to a French high admiral, and as a token of respect all the boats sailing past on the Gironde used to lower their sails (*baisse-voile*). This became corrupted to the present name.

Off to the left is Château Lagrange, which though classified in l855, had fallen on hard times until it was purchased in1983 by the Japanese whisky group, Suntory. They have spent millions of francs in restoring the vineyards, the press-house and cellars and the château.

Pauillac

Châteaux Lagrange and Beychevelle have the *appellation* Saint-Julien – one that they share with many of the finest wines of Bordeaux, though none of them are classified as first growths. The town of Pauillac though, has three first growths: Mouton-Rothschild, Latour and Lafite-Rothschild.

In the 1855 classification, Mouton was only rated as a second growth. For more than a century it was in a rather ambivalent position, for it considered itself to be a first growth in all but name. In a bid to strengthen its position it used to charge as much as, and sometimes more than, the first growths.

This led to an unfortunate leapfrogging situation and a price-spiral. In fact it took a ministerial decree, in 1973, to confirm its status as a *premier cru*.

Château Latour, which has a reputation for producing the firmest wine of the first growths, stands on a low hill to the south of the village. It has a highly-rated second wine called Les Forts de Latour.

The vineyard takes its name from a 19th-century tower standing by the château, which is reputed to have been built from a fort that previously stood on the site.

Château Lafite-Rothschild is a beautiful château standing in a lovely park on the northern boundaries of Pauillac. (Note that visits should be arranged through the château's Paris office.) Beyond lies the last of the village appellations of the Haut-Médoc, Saint-Estèphe.

Saint-Estèphe

While Pauillac may give the fullest wines, Margaux the most delicate, and Saint-Julien the richest, those of Saint-Estèphe have the tendency to be the most austere, they take some time to soften out and become great wines.

Perhaps the best-known wine of the village is Château Cos d'Estournel, which has a striking position on a small hill on the right-hand side of the road. Striking the architecture certainly is, for there is no other château quite like this in all Bordeaux.

To build one's cow-sheds in the form of an oriental folly must have taken some imagination – and a lot of money. This is exactly what Louis Gaspard d'Estournel, the then owner, did 170 years ago.

Château Mouton Rothschild 33250 Pauillac. Tel: 05 56 73 21 29. Fax: 05 56 73 21 28. (Mlle Parinet). Apr-Oct every day, Nov-Mar Mon-Fri, 0930-1100, 1400-1600 (Fri 1500). By guided tour only, visits start 0930, 1100, 1400, 1530. T.P.E.G. ☎

Château Pichon-Longueville Baron 33250 Pauillac. Tel: 05 56 73 17 17. Fax: 05 56 73 17 28. (M. Matignon). Every day 0900-1130, 1400-1700. *Son et lumière* display Fri 2100-2230. T.F.W.S.E.G.S. ☎ www.pichonlongueville.com

Château Pichon-Longueville Ctesse. de Lalande 33250 Pauillac. Tel: 05 56 59 19 40. Fax: 05 56 59 29 78. Mon-Fri 0900-1130, 1400-1630. Sat 1000-1130, 1400-1630. Terrace with view over Gironde. By appointment only. E.G. ☎ www.pichon-lalande.com

ST.-ESTEPHE

Château Cos d'Estournel 33180 St.-Estèphe. Tel: 05 56 73 15 50. Fax: 05 56 59 72 59. Mon-Fri 1000-1200, 1400-1700. Closed Sat, Sun, hols. By appointment only (48 hours' written notice). T.F.E.

FOR FURTHER INFORMATION
Conseil des Vins du Médoc 1, cours du 30 Juillet, 33000 Bordeaux. Tel: 05 56 48 18 62. Fax: 05 56 79 11 05.

Maison du Tourisme et du Vin de Pauillac la Verrerie, 33250 Pauillac. Tel: 05 56 59 03 08. Fax: 05 56 59 23 38. Every day. Audio-visual presentation. T.P.W.S.E.G.I.

Maison du Vin de Margaux place la Trémoille, 33460 Margaux. Tel: 05 57 88 70 82. Fax: 05 57 88 38 27.

Maison du Vin de St.-Estèphe place de l'Eglise, 33180 St.-Estèphe. Tel: 05 56 59 30 59. Fax: 05 56 59 73 72. Jun, Sep. T.P (T.F with purchase) W.S.E.

If you turn left, just beyond Cos d'Estournel, you come to the small village of Cissac. While it has no classified growths in the 1855 table, there is little doubt that when a new table comes to be created it will have some candidates for the lower ranks.

The Haut-Médoc finishes at the northern boundary of Saint-Estèphe. To the north, the wines only have a right to the *appellation* Médoc.

The tower that gives its name to Château Latour at Pauillac, which many experts say produces the finest wine in Bordeaux.

Many of these are very sound wines. One vineyard that is of particular note is Château Loudenne, which was set up as a model estate during the last century by the Gilbey family. The property even had its own quay, so that the wine could be shipped direct to Britain.

The White Wines of Bordeaux

It was not very long ago that the white wines of Bordeaux were not being treated very seriously, but now all that has changed. The great sweet white wines have come back into fashion and modern wine-making techniques, and the Sauvignon grape, have created a new generation of crisp white wines. In the past, few of the wines could truly have been described as dry, but this is no longer the case.

There is some white wine made in most of the Bordeaux regions – even Château Margaux produces a little called Pavillon Blanc de Château Margaux – but the finest are produced upstream from Bordeaux on both banks of the Garonne.

The vineyards of the Graves close to Bordeaux are best known for their red wines, but as you drive south-west, parallel to the motorway on the N113, you move steadily into white wine country.

Château Carbonnieux, at Léognan, in fact produces slightly more red wine than white, but there

In every town, and most villages in France, the weekly market plays an important part in shopping.

is an amusing story about the latter. In the 18th century, the property belonged to the Benedictine monks of Sainte-Croix, and they were the first to plant white grapes. The story has it that a beautiful young girl from the region was captured by the Sultan of Constantinople and she introduced him to the wine, which, because of his religious principles, she called Carbonnieux Mineral Water. He became one of the monks' most regular customers!

Château de Labrède

A few kilometers further along at Labrède is the beautiful château, surrounded by a moat, where Montesquieu was born. This was rebuilt in 1429, on what remained of an earlier fortress.

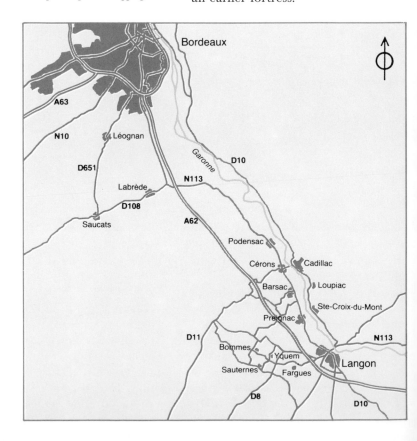

At the village of Podensac there is, by the side of the main road, the Maison des Vins de Graves, open every day in July, August and September, where information about the local wines can be obtained. Podensac is also the beginning of the area producing sweet white wines with the *appellation* Cérons.

Here the situation is slightly confused, for the local growers have the choice of making a dry white wine or a red wine that they can call Graves, or a sweet white wine called Cérons. At the moment, about four times as much dry wine is produced in the village as sweet.

The sweet white wines

To make a great sweet wine in Bordeaux is not an easy, or a cheap, process. It is achieved by picking the grapes late in the autumn, when they have been attacked by what is known as the noble rot, *Botrytis cinerea*. This feeds on the water in the grapes, but leaves the sugar. The resulting grape is shrivelled like a raisin, but extremely sweet.

Noble rot

Naturally, the yields are very low, for there is little juice in the grapes. The noble rot is encouraged by autumn mists and thus the greatest vineyards making this type of wine are nearly always close to water; in this case the Ciron or the Garonne rivers.

Indeed Botrytis is usually looked upon as an enemy to winemaking, as it is normally caused by rain. It is this particular combination of moisture from the mists and autumn sun that results in the greatest sweet white wines in the world. In all of these, the intense sweetness of the wine will be balanced by a certain acidity. It is this factor that enables these wines to age for fifty years or more.

At vintage time, the pickers will pass through the vineyards three or four times, just picking those grapes that have been affected by the rot.

There are three reasons, therefore, for the high cost of these wines: perfect, long warm falls are needed, yields are very low, and the vintages are labor intensive.

PORTETS
Château Rahoul 33640 Portets. Tel: 05 56 67 01 12. Fax: 05 56 67 02 88. By appointment only. Mon-Fri. TF.WS. ☎

PREIGNAC
Château Gilette 33210 Preignac. Tel: 05 56 76 28 44. Fax: 05 56 76 28 43. (M. and Mme Medeville). Mon-Thu 0900-1300, 1400-1800 (Fri 1700). Closed Aug. TF.WS.G.S E-mail: christian.medeville@ wanadoo.fr www.caves-particulières.com

SAINTE-CROIX-DU-MONT
The sweet wines of Ste.-Croix-du-Mont were once as highly prized as those of Sauternes, which lies on the opposite bank of the Garonne. The hill of Ste. Croix is reputed to be made up of fossilized oyster shells. In ancient times these were believed to give the wine aphrodisiac qualities. Be that as it may, many of these sweet wines still represent excellent value for money.

The beautiful Château de Labrède in the Graves, built in the 15th century and the birthplace of Montesquieu.

SAUTERNES
Château Suduiraut
33210 Preignac. Tel:
05 56 63 61 92. Fax:
05 56 63 61 93. Mon-Fri
0900-1200, 1400-1700.
Cellar visit. T.F.WS.E. ☎
www.suduiraut.com
Château Filhot 33210
Sauternes. Tel: 05 56 76 61
09. Fax: 05 56 76 67 91.
(M. Henri de Vaucelles).
Every day 0900-1900. TF
(with purchase). WS.E.G.S.
www.filhot.com
FOR FURTHER INFORMATION
Graves
Maison des Vins de
Graves RN 113, 33720
Podensac. Tel:
05 56 27 09 25. Fax:
05 56 27 17 36. T.F.WS.E.
The sweet white wines
Maison du Vin de
Sauternes place de la
Mairie, Sauternes, 33210
Langon. Tel: 05 56 76 69 83.
Fax: 05 56 76 69 67. WS.E.
Maison du Vin de Cadillac
Château des Ducs
d'Epernon, 33410 Cadillac.
Tel/Fax: 05 56 62 15 27.
Every day May-Oct.
TF.WS. (☎ for groups.)

Sauternes

The finest of these sweet wines are called Sauternes and they come from the vineyards of five small villages on the right of the main road. The first of these is Sauternes itself (from which comes the noble, and expensive, Château d'Yquem), Bommes, Fargues, Preignac and Barsac.

The wines from this last village can call themselves Barsac, rather than Sauternes. Barsac wines are generally considered to have rather less intense sweetness than the normal Sauternes, but rather more finesse.

Three varieties of grape are used in the manufacture of Sauternes: the Sémillon, normally about three-quarters of the whole; the Sauvignon, about a quarter; and traces of the Muscadelle.

Château d'Yquem

While everybody has their favorite Sauternes, it is generally considered that the finest is made at Château d'Yquem. As with the wines of the Haut-Médoc, those of the Sauternes were classified in 1855, and this was the only one to be rated *Premier Cru Supérieur.*

The château has belonged to the Lur-Saluces family since they obtained it by marriage in 1785. In 1999, it was bought by Moët Hennessy Louis Vuitton (L.V.M.H.), but Count Alexandre de Lur-Saluces, the sixth generation of the family at d'Yquem, remains in charge.

In poor years no wine will be sold as Château d'Yquem, but in some years a dry white wine is made called "Y" (pronounced "*ygrec*"). This is produced from 50 per cent Sauvignon grapes and 50 per cent Semillon – at Yquem there is no Muscadelle planted.

The yields for their Sauternes are so small that they like to say that each year they produce one glassful per vine!

There are a number of other great wines made including Coutet and Climens from Barsac; Rieussec at Fargues; Suduiraut at Preignac; and La Tour-Blanche at Bommes. This last belongs to the French Ministry of Agriculture and is run as a form of wine school for local, and other, growers.

One question is "When to drink Sauternes?" The French seem to like to drink it at the beginning of a meal and suggest that it is the ideal accompaniment for *foie gras*. For most of us that would certainly restrict the consumption! I feel that it is better at the end of a meal – it can go well with nuts or even certain strong cheeses like Roquefort.

Langon

The capital of the white wine district is Langon. Here, Claude Darroze is an excellent restaurant, which also has reasonably priced rooms. One can then either return to Bordeaux directly by the motorway, or cross over the Garonne and return via the vineyard areas on the other bank. A third possibility is to drive south on the D392 to the vineyards of Armagnac.

A traditional part of the cookery of the Bordeaux region is grilling over a fire of vine-shoots. This gives the meat a distinctive taste. Here, the chef at the Grillobois at Cérons turns the steaks.

Entre Deux Mers

The vast area between the Garonne and Dordogne rivers is known as the Entre Deux Mers, "between two seas." It claims to be the largest single *appellation contrôlée* in France. Here, the growers have decided that their future lies in making clean, dry white wines. Their red has to be called Bordeaux or Bordeaux Supérieur.

It is a region of rolling countryside with small villages. In the south there are a number of fortified mills. There are also market towns established by the English, like Sauveterre de Guyenne. This is a gentle area off the normal routes.

Premières Côtes de Bordeaux

The D10, along the east bank of the Garonne, is a pretty route between the river and vineyard slopes producing, for the most part, sweet white wine. Much of this is sold as Premières Côtes de Bordeaux. There are, however, three smaller areas, each with a right to its own *appellation*: Cadillac, Sainte-Croix-du-Mont and Loupiac, sometimes described as "the poor man's Sauternes."

For long these wines were out of fashion and the growers were in despair. It is pleasant to see that the tide has turned and they are coming into their own once again.

The finest wine demands the finest cask. A cooper in the Sauternais prepares on oak cask for ageing the local wine.

APPELLATION SAUTERNES CONTROLÉE

CHATEAU DE FARGUES
Lur Saluces
SAUTERNES
—— 1983 ——
750ml   MIS EN BOUTEILLE AU CHATEAU
LUR-SALUCES FARGUES DE LANGON (GDE) FRANCE

Bourg and Blaye

Tasting the red wines at Château Tayac at Bourg. Most vineyards welcome visitors, but not many have such well-developed tasting facilities as this.

BOURG
Château Tayac St. Seurin de Bourg, 33719 Bourg sur Gironde. Tel: 05 57 68 40 60. Fax: 05 57 68 29 93. Mon-Fri 1000-1200, 1400-1800. Sat, Sun by appointment. Panoramic views of Gironde estuary. TF.WS.E. ☎ (☎ Sat, Sun).

BLAYE
Château Peybonhomme-les-Tours 33390 Cars. Tel: 05 57 42 11 95. Fax: 05 57 42 38 15. Mon-Sat 1000-1200, 1400-1800. Sun by appointment only. Small museum in tower. Panoramic views of Gironde estuary. Tasting cellar. TF.WS.E. ☎ E-mail: peybonhomme@terre-net.fr
FOR FURTHER INFORMATION
Maison du Vin de Bourg place de l'Eperon, 33710 Bourg. Tel: 05 57 94 80 20. Fax: 05 57 94 80 21. G. www.bourg.cotes-bordeaux. alienor.fr

There are few who would claim that the vineyards of Bordeaux are beautiful. There are beautiful châteaux and there is some agreeable countryside, but if it were not for the wines, there are few places where one would drive just for the view. One of the exceptions is in the region of Bourg and Blaye.

Bourg is a pleasant town, which for nearly a year during the siege of Bordeaux in the 17th century was the seat of the French court. The road from there leads along the bank of the river at the foot of chalky cliffs. There are wonderful views across the flat islands in the river to the Haut-Médoc and its châteaux.

The town of Blaye is dominated by the citadel, which was built by Vauban to command the approaches to the Gironde, together with Fort-Médoc at Cussac, and Fort Pâté on a small island in the middle of the river. The strategic importance of Blaye had been recognized by the Romans who built a fort there. Gastronomically, it has some importance as it is the center of a limited caviar industry.

To the north of Blaye, the vineyards finish, as the land turns into a sandy marsh. Here there is a nuclear power station looking across the river to Saint-Estèphe.

Before the planting of the vineyards in the Médoc, it was those of Bourg and Blaye that made the reputation of the wines of Bordeaux. Now they concentrate on producing light, early-maturing red wines, with a lot of fruit, and clean, dry white wines. Much of the latter is turned into sparkling wine by a large producer outside Bourg.

The countryside is very pretty, much hillier than most of Bordeaux, consisting largely of a series of rolling ridges, running parallel to the river topped with attractive little châteaux – the better wines seem to come from those closer to the river. For the lover of churches, there are a number in the area that date back to before the time of the English occupation.

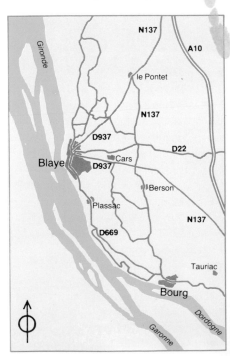

Pomerol

The vineyards of Pomerol form an angled square, with one corner in the center of the old wine port of Libourne (which is today better known for its excellent food market). Each side of the square measures no more than 3km (2 miles), so the area is small.

There were vineyards here in Roman times and the viticultural tradition was maintained by the Knights of St. John of Jerusalem, who built a manor house, a hospital and a church in the neighborhood.

Pétrus

The small scale of the vineyard properties, taken together with increasing demand from around the world, means that certain wines from Pomerol are now the most expensive in all Bordeaux.

Even the most famous, Pétrus (for some reason the word "Château" is usually dropped from its name) produces no more than 160 casks in an average vintage, less than a sixth of Château Latour, for example.

The Pomerol vineyards

The village of Pomerol itself scarcely features even on a large-scale road map, and the individual vineyards are scattered around all over the area – many of the "châteaux" seemingly only unassuming farmhouses.

Pomerol's vineyards are split in two by the N89, which follows the route of an old Roman road.

To the west of this road, the soil has a sandy base, and this gives wines that are lighter and rather lacking in character.

Château Peybonhomme-les-Tours in the Blayais is typical of many of the properties in Bordeaux, with a variety of architectural styles developed over the centuries.

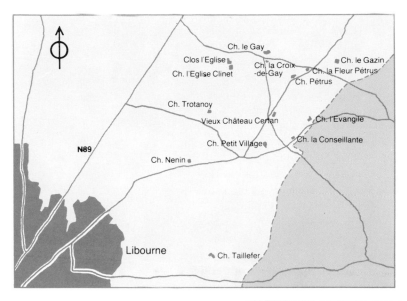

All the finest wines come from the eastern side of the road, where the gravelly soil gives them much more "backbone."

Here, the Merlot is the dominant grape variety, and it gives a wine that is believed by some to resemble the wines of Burgundy, for it has a rich, velvety taste not found elsewhere in Bordeaux.

POMEROL
Château la Croix de Gay/
Château la Fleur de Gay
Pomerol, 33500 Libourne. Tel: 05 57 51 19 05. Fax: 05 57 74 15 62. Mon-Thu, Sat, 0900-1200, 1330-1800. Closed Fri, Sun. T.F.WS.E.
Château Petit Village
Pomerol, 33500 Libourne. Tel: 05 57 51 21 08. Fax: 05 57 51 87 31. T.F.WS. ☎

Saint-Emilion

If I were asked to nominate the three most complete wine towns in France, they would be Beaune, in Burgundy; Riquewihr, in Alsace; and St.-Emilion. Coincidentally, each of them has a compactness given by town walls. Perhaps it is these that have helped to preserve, and concentrate, the character in each case.

Much of St.-Emilion's history is recalled in the names of many of the châteaux. The vineyards were first planted by the Romans, and the poet Ausonius (who also appreciated the wines of the Moselle) is supposed to have found his wife in Bordeaux and to have lived in St.-Emilion. His name is remembered in the great wines of Château Ausone.

For a time the region was occupied by the Moors (Château Villemaurine) and then became an important ecclesiastical center, as indicated by such names as Château le Couvent, which is actually within the town walls, Clos la Madeleine and Clos de l'Oratoire.

It is not easy to decide what to advise the visitor to see in the town. There are the underground church and the catacombs, the Couvent des Jacobins, the Collegiate Church, with its beautiful cloisters, the town walls and the cave retreat of the 8th-century St. Aemilianus, who gave his name to the town. For those who want to have

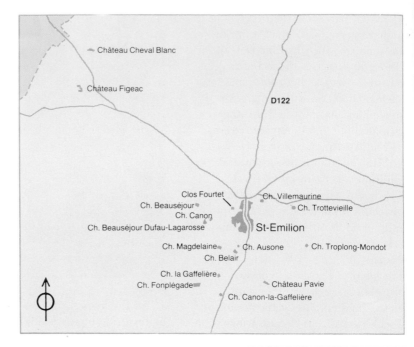

History underfoot

St.-Emilion did a brisk trade in wine with Britain in the 17th and 18th centuries. Ships sailed from Bristol, laden with stones as ballast. These were then left at the small port of Vignonet on the Dordogne river. This accounts for the fact that St.-Emilion's streets are still paved with granite and other rock varieties from Wales and Cornwall.

the decision taken out of their hands, regular guided tours on foot leave the tourist office in the Place des Créneaux throughout the year.

The *appellation* St.-Emilion includes a host of châteaux, with vineyards, in eight communes, on three distinct types of soil, and, therefore, of three distinct qualities. Perhaps surprisingly, the final decision as to which villages could call their wine St.-Emilion came as late as 1929, and was based on rights granted in 1289.

The first of the vineyard types is the continuation of the plateau with its chalky soil, rich in iron, of the vineyards of Pomerol. Here the two outstanding châteaux are Cheval Blanc and Figeac.

Around the town itself, the plateau falls away to the plain. On the slopes, where the soil is similar, are the vineyards of the Côtes, with ideal exposure to the south-east. Here, the château with the highest reputation is Ausone, followed by Belair, Pavie and la Gaffelière.

ST.-EMILION
Dubois-Challon Château Belair, 33300 St.-Emilion. Tel: 05 57 24 70 94. Fax: 05 57 24 67 11. (Madeleine Delbeck). 1000-1200, 1400-1800. By appointment only. Historic cellars. TF.WS.E.G. ☎
Consorts Valette Château Pavie, 33330 St-Emilion. Tel: 05 57 55 43 43. Fax: 05 57 24 63 99. (Open to public after harvest). Mon-Fri 0930-1200, 1430-1700. TP.E. ☎
www.chateaupavie.com

FRONSAC
S.A. du Château de la Rivière 33126 Fronsac. Tel: 05 57 55 56 56. Fax: 05 57 24 94 39. 0900-1130, 1400-1700 15 Jun-15 Sep, every day. 16 Sep-14 Jun, Mon-Fri only. TF (with purchase). WS.E. ☎
www.chateau-de-la-riviere.com

Down on the plain, where the soil is a mixture of sand and gravel, the quality of the wine can be distinctly inferior, yet it still benefits from the name St.-Emilion. Perhaps because of this weakness, there has developed an immensely complicated system of classification. The two top classifications are *St.-Emilion Premier Grand Cru Classé* and *St.-Emilion Grand Cru Classé*. These are re-assessed every ten years. At present there are 13 within the first category – though two of them, Ausone and Cheval Blanc, are given a higher rating within the category – and 55 in the second.

In addition, each year, any vineyard can send its wine to be sampled and, if it is found worthy, it is given the status of *Grand Cru* for that particular vintage. This means that in any given year, there may be hundreds of such wines,

some scarcely of a quality that their classification would suggest.

Most St.-Emilion is made from the Merlot and Cabernet Franc grapes. At its best it is one of the most satisfying wines of Bordeaux, having a rich fruitiness that appeals to those put off by the austerity of many Médoc wines.

Surrounding the vineyards of Pomerol and St.-Emilion, there are a number of areas producing similar wines. Indeed, before the coming of *appellation contrôlée*, much of the wine used to be sold under their names, and some of these areas have since gained reflected glory by adding one or the other name to their own. These areas include Lalande de Pomerol, Lussac-St.-Emilion, St.-Georges-St.-Emilion, Puisseguin-St.-Emilion, Montagne-St.-Emilion, Fronsac, Canon Fronsac and Côtes de Castillon.

FOR FURTHER INFORMATION
Syndicat Viticole et Agricole de St.-Emilion B.P.15, 33330 St.-Emilion. Tel: 05 57 55 50 50. Fax: 05 57 55 53 10. (Not open to the general public).
Maison du Vin de St.-Emilion place Pierre Meyrat, 33330 St.-Emilion. Tel: 05 57 55 50 55. Fax: 05 57 55 53 10. WS.E. Every day 0930-1230, 1400-1830.
Maison des Vins de Fronsac plaisance, 33126 Fronsac. Tel: 05 57 51 80 51. Fax: 05 57 25 98 19. TF Jul, Aug only. WS.E.

The vineyards of the historic town of St.-Emilion even break through its walls in some places. To the left is the Norman-style castle, built by Louis VIII.

Bergerac and Cahors

BERGERAC
Domaine du Haut Pécharmant
Pécharmant, 24100 Bergerac.
Tel: 05 53 57 29 50. Fax:
05 53 24 28 05. (M. Roches).
Every day 0800-1200, 1400-
1900. Picnic area, camp site.
TF.WS.S. (☎ for groups.)
Château de Monbazillac
Monbazillac, 242420
Sigoulès. Tel: 05 53 61 52 52.
Cellars Mon-Sat. Jul-Aug
1830-1230, 1330-1900.
Sep-Jun 1000-1230, 1330-
1900. Chateau 1000-1930.
Shop. TF. ☎
www.monbazillac.com

FOR FURTHER INFORMATION
Bergerac
C.I.V.R.B. 2, place du Dr.
Cayla, 24104 Bergerac.
Tel: 05 53 63 57 55. TF
(TP ☎ for groups) WS.E.
E-mail: vin.civb@wanadoo.fr
Cahors
Union Interprofessionel
du Vin de Cahors
Maison du Vin, B.P. 61,
430 ave Jean-Jaurès, 46002
Cahors. Tel: 05 65 23 22 24.
Fax: 05 65 23 22 27.

In the Middle Ages, most of the wine that was shipped from Bordeaux came not from the local vineyards, but from what was called the *Haut-Pays*, up the Dordogne and the Garonne and their tributaries. Today, there are still wines from those regions, with the best probably coming from around Bergerac on the Dordogne and Cahors on the Lot.

Bergerac

The vineyards of Bergerac are a logical continuation of those of Bordeaux, and they produce a range of wines that are remarkably similar. The finest dry white wines come from the vineyards of Montravel, on both sides of the main road from Bordeaux and Libourne, to the west of Sainte-Foy-la-Grande.

The finest sweet wines, produced in the same way and from the same grapes as Sauternes, come from around the town of Monbazillac, to the south of Bergerac.

The local red wines are similar to the lighter clarets, with the finest having the *appellation* Pécharmant.

Cahors

The town of Cahors is built on and around a rock in a sweeping bend in the river Lot. Its most striking feature is the fortified Valentré bridge, built five hundred years ago. It is the center of the gastronomic region of Quercy, long reputed for its walnuts and its truffles.

The basic grape of Cahors is the Malbec, here called the Auxerrois, which plays a supporting role in Bordeaux. Traditional methods of vinification used to give what was known as a "black" wine, deep in color, full of tannin and long-lasting.

Modern wine-making methods and more planting in the sandy valley floor, rather than on the limestone slopes, now give rather lighter, but by no means light, wines, which mature earlier.

The Château of Monbazillac, which now belongs to the local co-operative cellar and houses a restaurant and museum.

Armagnac

After Cognac, the second great brandy of France is Armagnac. This comes from a region to the south-east of Bordeaux. As in Cognac, there are distinctive vineyard regions: to the east and south, the hilly Haut-Armagnac; in the middle, centered on Condom, the Ténarèze; and to the west, the sandy-soiled Bas-Armagnac. It is from this last that the most renowned spirits come. In some ways Armagnac might be said to be a country cousin to Cognac and indeed they are related – some of the more important Armagnac companies now belong to Cognac houses.

It is, however, an area of small producers selling an individual product. There appears to be a measure of pragmatism as to the method of distillation, but the traditional Armagnac is still a hybrid between the pot still of Cognac and malt whisky, and the continuous patent still of grain whisky.

Distillation

The spirit is distilled only once and comes off the still at a relatively low strength, thus having in it a higher proportion of congenerics, or flavors. It is then aged in casks made from the local oak, which naturally imparts a great deal of color and softens the spirit more rapidly than does the wood used for ageing Cognac. Most Armagnac is then put into the distinctive regional bottle, the *gasconne*.

Is it better than Cognac? That is a matter of personal taste. It is a bit like asking, "Is Burgundy better than claret?" Some like one, some like the other, and many like both. Armagnac tends to be more flavorsome and, perhaps, less smooth. It will appeal to the person who is looking for something different after a meal.

There is also a local aperitif, *floc de Gascogne*, similar to *Pineau des Charentes*.

CONDOM
Armagnac Janneau 50 ave de la Gare, 32100 Condom. Tel: 05 62 28 24 77. Fax: 05 62 28 48 00. (Mr Phillips). Mon-Fri 0900-1200, 1400-1700. Museum. T.F.WS.E.I.S. E-mail: janneau@wanadoo.fr
Armagnac Larressingle Papelorey S.A. rue des Carmes, 32100 Condom. Tel: 05 62 28 15 33. Fax: 05 62 28 36 99. (M. Papelorey). Mon-Fri 0830-1200, 1300-1600. Closed 1st. fortnight in Aug. Cellar visit. T.F.WS.E.S.
EAUZE
Château du Tariquet P. Grassa Fille et Fils, 32800 Eauze. Tel: 05 62 09 87 82. Fax: 05 62 09 89 49. By appointment only. Armagnac and *vin de pays*. T.F.WS.S. ☎ www.tariquet.com
GONDRIN-COURRENSAN
Armagnac Veuve Goudoulin Clos du Presbytère, rte de Vic-Fezensac, 32330 Courrensan. Tel: 05 62 06 35 02. Fax: 05 62 06 59 46. Mon-Fri 0900-1200, 1400-1800. Vintage Armagnacs. T.F.WS.
VIC-FEZENSAC
Ets. Gelas et Fils 32190 Vic-Fezensac. Tel: 05 62 06 30 11. Fax: 05 62 06 58 95. (M. Philippe Gelas or Mme Nathalie Goma). Mon-Fri 0900-1200, 1400-1800. Armagnacs, single estate Bas-Armagnac range and *Eau de Vie* from plums. T.F.WS.E.G.S. www.gelas.com
FOR FURTHER INFORMATION
B.N.I.A. Place de la Liberté, 32800 Eauze. Tel: 05 62 08 11 00. Fax: 05 62 08 11 01. S. E-mail: armagnac.bureau. national@wanadoo.fr

Casks ageing in the cellars of Janneau – to many people the best-known name of Armagnac.

The South-West

BUZET
Les Vignerons de Buzet
B.P. 17, 47160 Buzet-sur-
Baïse. Tel: 05 53 84 74 30.
Fax: 05 53 84 74 24. Mon-
Fri 0900-1230, 1400-1900
(1800 in winter). TF.WS.E.
www.vignerons-buzet.fr

FRONTON
Château Bellevue la
Forêt rte D49, 31620
Fronton. Tel: 05 61 82 43 21.
Fax: 05 61 82 39 70. Mon-
Sat 0900-1200, 1400-1800.
TF.WS.E. E-mail:
chateau.bellevue@ wanadoo.fr
www.chateaubelluelaforet.com

GAILLAC
Cave de Labastide
Labastide de Lévis, 81150
Marssac. Tel: 05 63 53 73 73.
Fax: 05 63 53 73 74. Mon-
Thu 0900-1200, 1400-
1800. Fri 0900-1200, 1400-
1700 TF.WS.G.I.

Château Lastours
H.&P. de Faramond,
81310 Lisle-sur-Tarn. Tel:
05 63 57 07 09. Fax:
05 63 41 01 95. Every day
0900-1200, 1400-1800.
Historic château.
TF.WS.E.

JURANCON
Caves des Producteurs
de Jurançon 53, ave
Henri IV, 64290 Gan. Tel:
05 59 21 57 03. Fax:
05 59 21 72 06. Mon-Sat
0800-1300, 1330-1930. Jul-
Aug only, Sun 0930-1230,
1500-1900. TF.WS.E.
E-mail: cave.gan@adour-
bureau.fr www.pageszoom.
com/cave-jurancon

MADIRAN
Domaine Pichard
Soublecause, 65700
Maubourguet. Tel:
05 62 96 35 73. Fax:
05 62 96 96 72. (M.
Tachouères). Mon-Fri
0900-1200, 1400-1730.
TF.WS.E. ☎

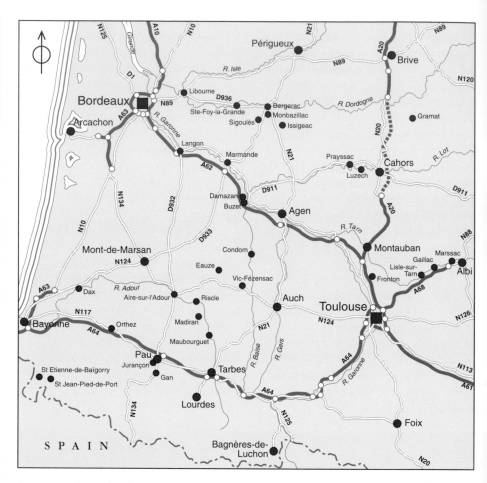

In many places in the south-west of France there are small vineyard areas with either *appellation contrôlée* or VDQS status that are striving to better their reputation. In some cases, the move may be led by a single dedicated grower, in others most of the production may be in the hands of a co-operative cellar. In either case, local wine-making might have come to an end but for these efforts.

The region is crossed by two motorways running almost parallel. To the north, there is the A62, then the A61, which joins Bordeaux to Toulouse and the Mediterranean; to the south, the A64 running from Bayonne to Toulouse via Pau and Tarbes. Many of the small vineyard regions lie close to these motorways and can make for a short but interesting diversion.

Some 80km (50 miles) from Bordeaux, on the A62, the vineyards of the Côtes du Marmandais lie to the left. Here, a variety of Bordeaux and local grapes go to make easy-drinking red wines.

More serious are those of Buzet, produced on the south bank of the Garonne in the 30km (20 miles) before Agen. The best wines from the local co-operative cellar have shown well against wines from Bordeaux in blind tastings.

On the left of the motorway, before Toulouse, is the small town of Fronton, around which are made fruity red wines with a basis of the Négrette grape. The largest property in the area is the ambitious Château Bellevue la Forêt.

Gaillac

Further to the north-east is the important historical vineyard region of Gaillac. Here are made red, white, rosé and slightly sparkling wines from a very broad range of grape varieties. There is a mixture of qualities, probably depending on the ingredients, but there are some excellent red and rosé wines.

Madiran

The wine that is most often drunk in the restaurants of the Armagnac region comes from the south. This is Madiran, made largely from the Tannat grape. Rather rough and ready when young, it develops with ageing into an excellent, full-bodied wine.

The local white wine is the Pacherenc de Vic Bilh. This has an intense flavor and is made, according to the vintage, in a variety of degrees of sweetness.

Also made in the area is a little Béarn, in red, white and rosé, though most of it is produced to the south, west of the town of Pau.

Jurançon

In the nineteenth century, the view of the mountains from the Boulevard des Pyrénées in Pau was considered by the large British expatriate community to be one of the finest in Europe. The castle is worth a visit, and there is a museum on the top floor.

Here the finest white wine is Jurançon (yet another wine to use the ubiquitous Henri IV in its publicity). The story goes that he was actually baptized with it.

Jurançon used to be a sweet wine, picked late to obtain the maximum amount of sugar in the grapes. Although 75% of today's production is Jurançon Sec – a steely dry wine – the sweet variety, which is capable of ageing for many years, has now come back into fashion.

Irouléguy

Finally, from the Basque country, there are the reds, rosés and whites of Irouléguy. Here, around the beautiful town of Saint-Jean-Pied-de-Port, the vineyard area was, until recently, reduced to just 90 hectares (215 acres), with all the wine being made by one co-operative cellar.

However, ambitious plans by a number of local growers have led to a further 50 hectares (about 125 acres) being planted on the steep hillsides.

IROULEGUY
Domaine Brana Ispoure, 64220 St.-Jean-Pied-de-Port. Tel: 05 59 37 00 44. Fax: 05 59 37 14 28. (M. and Mme Brana). Distillery: Mon-Fri 0900-1200, 1400-1800 (closed last 2 weeks Jan). Vineyard: Jul, Aug every day 1000-1200, 1430-1800. T.F.WS.E.S.

FOR FURTHER INFORMATION

C.I.V.S.O. B.P.18, 31321 Castanet-Tolosan. Tel: 05 61 73 87 06; Fax: 05 61 75 64 39. E-mail: civso@vins-du-sud-ouest.com www. vins-du-sud-ouest.com

A peaceful scene in the Basque town of St.-Jean-Pied-de-Port, in the foothills of the Pyrénées, not far from the Spanish frontier.

Languedoc-Roussillon

The vine has long been central to the economic life of the Midi, which is France's oldest wine-growing area. Narbonne along with Marseilles was one of the first places where the Greeks planted vines back in the 6th century B.C. In parts of the Midi the vine is the only viable crop, able to survive in the thin soils of the hills and the long dry summers.

Despite all the recent plantings throughout the world, the swathe of vines that runs from the Rhône valley down to the Spanish border near Banyuls remains the largest vineyard in the world. It is also now one of the most dynamic in Europe.

To get to Languedoc-Roussillon
Montpellier is 759 km (472 miles) from Paris via the A10, A71, A75 and N109. It is 109 km (68 miles) from Orange by the A6, A7 and A9. Narbonne is 386 km (240 miles) from Bordeaux via A62 and A61. Perpignan is 854 km (530 miles) from Paris (A10, A71, A75 and A9).

Thirty years ago, when the average wine consumption in France was over 100 liters (25 gallons) a head, the Midi produced oceans of cheap, thin red wine (*gros rouge*) to supply the home thirst. Until Algerian independence these thin wines were bolstered by beefy Algerian wine. They were thin because the yields were enormously high.

Since then, French drinking patterns have changed radically and the Midi has changed beyond recognition. The accent is now on quality. The region now produces some of the most exciting and best value wines in France.

Head for the hills

In the vast plains of Languedoc, a new form of industrialized vine growing has replaced the old production of *gros rouge*. Instead of Aramon and Alicante Bouchet, which provided French workers with their *vin ordinaire*, now it is Chardonnay, Merlot and Cabernet Sauvignon that are planted on the plain. During the last fifteen years there has been a lot of investment in these vineyards by French wine companies based in other parts of France, such as Bordeaux and Burgundy, and by companies from Australia and California.

Vins de Pays

Most of these wines are sold as *vin de pays*, usually as single varietal wines. Cabernet Sauvignon, Merlot, Syrah and Chardonnay are the most popular varieties. The archaic French legislation now allows producers to name two varieties on the label, but under no circumstances are they allowed to mention three! The *vin de pays* denomination is also used by growers in *appellation contrôlée* areas who have grape varieties that do not fit into the over-rigid French appellation rules.

At the end of the 1980s, James Herrick raised eyebrows both in the region and amongst traditionalists in Britain by planting 170 hectares (420 acres) of Chardonnay a little to the north-west of Narbonne. He and his partners were among the first outside investors to spot the potential of the Languedoc. His neatly trellised vines with drip feed irrigation were an extraordinary contrast to the local tradition of straggly bush vines.

A more recent investor in the region is the well-known Chablis grower and merchant, Michel Laroche. He has bought and renovated a property close to Béziers called Domaine la Chevalière and is making *vin de pays* varietal wines.

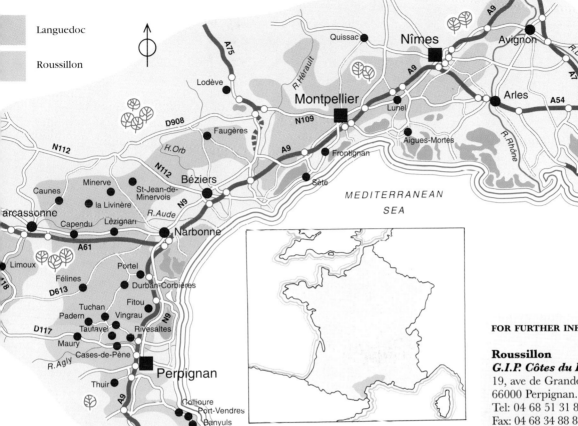

Languedoc

Roussillon

The Midi is also famous for the production of aperitifs such as Dubonnet, St. Raphael and Noilly Prat. The cellars of Noilly Prat in Marseillan are well worth a visit (see page 114 for visiting details). The Vermouth is aged outside in wooden barrels, so that it matures in the heat. A number of producers in Languedoc make Cathagène, which is a local version of Pineau de Charentes. Eau de Vie de Marc is added to grape juice, often from Grenache Blanc, but other varieties can be used, and the blend is then aged in barrel.

The Coteaux

Although it is interesting to see the developments on the plain, the visitor will find the real excitement in the hills that lie between the plain and the Cevennes mountains. Head for places like the Haut-Corbières, Minervois, Faugères, St. Chinian, Montpeyroux or Pic St. Loup.

Here much of the scenery is spectacular, with patches of vines interspersed by *garrigue*, the local name for the dry, scrubby bush that covers the hills. You find small villages either perched on the side of steep hillsides or wedged in between ravines. These hills are a world away from the busy beaches that fringe the Mediterranean, and are well worth exploring.

Most of the wine is red and it is usually made from a blend of Mediterranean varieties. Carignan is the traditional grape of the hills.

FOR FURTHER INFORMATION

Roussillon
G.I.P. Côtes du Roussillon
19, ave de Grande Bretagne, 66000 Perpignan.
Tel: 04 68 51 31 81.
Fax: 04 68 34 88 88. G.S.
www.vins-du-roussillon.com

Languedoc
Conseil Interprofessionnel des Vins du Languedoc
9 Cours Mirabeau, 11100 Narbonne. Tel: 04 68 90 38 30.
Fax: 04 68 32 38 00.

Syndicat des Vignerons Coteaux du Languedoc
Domaine de Maurin, Mas de Saporta, 34970 Lattes.
Tel: 04 67 06 04 44. Fax: 04 67 58 05 15.

WINE FESTIVALS
Faugères Fête du Grand St Jean: 1st Sunday in July
Narbonne Spring wine fair, end Apr.
Trausse-Minervois Wine festival, 1st two weeks of July.
Minerve Wine festival, last two weeks of July.

113

Vintaging in the Languedoc. The pickers empty their small baskets into the hotte, *the large one on the back of the man on the left. He then empties this into the trailer.*

BERLOU
Cave "Coteaux de Rieu-Berlou" 34360 Berlou. Tel: 04 67 89 58 58. Fax: 04 67 89 59 21. Mon-Sat 0900-1200, 1400-1800. T.F.E.

BEZIERS
Domaine de Chevalière
Route de Murviel, 34500 Béziers. Tel: 03 86 42 89 00. Fax: 03 86 42 89 29. Every day 0900-1200, 1330-1730.

CAUNES-MINERVOIS
Abbaye de Caunes
11160 Caunes-Minervois. Tel: 04 68 78 09 44. Every day 1000-1900. Cellars in 16th-century abbey. T.F.WS.E.G.S.

Clos Centeilles
Campagne de Centeilles, 34210 Siran. Tel: 04 68 91 52 18. Fax: 04 68 91 65 92. (Patricia and Daniel Domergue). Mon-Fri 1000-1200, 1600-1800. Minervois. T.F.WS.E. ☎

LA LIVINIERE
La Cave des Coteaux du Haut Minervois
34210 La Livinière. Tel: 04 68 91 42 67. Fax: 04 68 91 51 77. Jun-Aug, Mon-Fri, 0800-1200, 1400-1800, Sat 0800-1200, 1500-1900, Sun 0900-1200. Rest of year closed Sat pm, Sun. T.F.WS.

MARSEILLAN
Noilly Prat 34340 Marseillan. Tel: 04 67 77 20 15. Fax: 04 67 77 32 22. Every day 1000-1200, 1430-1800. Vermouth. T.P.WS.E.

From low yielding, old vines it produces full bodied, tannic wine. Grenache is used to give soft body and alcohol. More recently Syrah and Mourvèdre have been planted to improve the quality of the wines.

Coteaux de Languedoc
This is the general appellation for the eastern part of Languedoc. It covers wine in all three colors. A number of specific areas can add their local names to the appellation such as Pic St. Loup, Monteyroux and La Clape. In time, many of these areas will probably have their own separate appellations, as Faugères and St. Chinian have since 1982.

Pic St. Loup
The Pic is an impressive limestone rock some 20 km (12 miles) north of Montpellier. Because of the height, the distance from the sea and the cooling influence of the Cevennes Mountains, the wines here have more finesse and elegance than those of the plains. Over the past ten years Pic St.

Loup has established a reputation as one of the best areas for red wine in the Languedoc and, more recently, has been making some very impressive whites as well. The reds are chiefly made from Syrah, which particularly likes the cooler climate and makes wines that are closest to those of the Northern Rhône, though always with the herbal spice of the local *garrigue*.

Faugères
This elongated appellation is in the hills to the north of Béziers. AC Faugères runs east to west and encompasses a number of pretty little villages like Fos, Roquessels, Lenthéric and La Liquière. The soil is schist and vines share this hilly area with the *garrigue*. Some of the best wines from the Midi come from here, often with a high proportion of Syrah, which grows very successfully here. These are attractive hillside vineyards and it is worth taking the time to explore this area and enjoy the landscape.

St. Chinian

The St. Chinian appellation follows directly on to the west from Faugères. Like Faugères, the appellation is for red and rosé only. Whites come under the Coteaux du Languedoc. However, both are likely to be allowed to have their own ACs for whites in the future.

The first small town of any consequence is the very picturesque Roquebrun, whose center is built on a steep hillside overlooking the river Orb. A few miles west of Roquebrun is the co-operative of Berlou, which is among the best run in the Midi.

In the center of St. Chinian, on the Ave de la Promenade, is the Maison des Vins. Here you can taste and buy wines from St. Chinian as well as obtain information about the appellation and its producers.

Minervois

Driving south-west of St. Chinian, you come to St. Jean de Minervois, well known for its fortified Muscat, and then the extraordinary town of Minerve, which is built in a canyon where two gorges meet. It has had a bloody past. In 1210, during the religious wars against the Cathars, Simon de Montfort besieged the town and slaughtered most of the population.

Nowadays the area is more peaceful and is the highest part of AC Minervois, which became an appellation in 1985. Minervois can come in all three colors, but most are red. The Minervois is shaped like an enormous amphitheater facing south toward the flat valley of the Aude. From the heights around Minerve the vineyards cover a series of terraces that descend toward the Aude.

The quality of the wines from the Minervois has greatly improved over

The Château of Peyrepertuse, one of the last strongholds of the Cathar heretics who defended their faith against the Catholic Church in the 13th century.

the past ten years. Recently the area around La Livinière has been recognized as having some of the best vineyards, so La Livinière can now append its village name to the Minervois appellation. The high reputation of this area is due to the

PRADES-SUR-VERNAZOBRE
Alain Jougla Domaine de Jougla, 34360 Prades-sur-Vernazobre (St. Chinian). Tel: 04 67 38 06 02. Fax: 04 67 38 17 74. Open every day except Sun p.m. 0900-1200, 1400-1800. T.F.E.

High up in the hills of Languedoc, the wine of St. Chinian is produced, where, as the sign says, it can be tasted in 50 cellars in 20 different villages.

work of Maurice Piccinini, who has now retired. His son now runs Domaine Piccinini in the center of the village.

Recently a number of producers have been making a sweet late harvest wine here.

The Maison de Minervois is in the village of Siran and is a good source of information about the appellation and the producers. In the same grounds, the restaurant La Villa d'Eleis offers an interesting range of local wines.

Corbières and Fitou

This is an extraordinarily varied area. AC Corbières runs from the flat vineyards around Narbonne, close to the Mediterranean and the valley of the Aude, especially around Lezignan-Corbières, to the remote hills in the southern Corbières around the village of Cucugnan and the extraordinary Château de Peyrepertuse, on the border with Roussillon. In addition to visiting vineyards, this is a fascinating area to tour.

Although the Haut-Corbières is very attractive, some of the best wine comes from the lower land in the north around the village of Boutenac.

Château la Voulte-Gasparets is the best property in this sector.

Fitou, which became an AC in 1948, is the oldest red wine appellation in the Midi. It is formed of two separate enclaves within Corbières. The coastal enclave is around the village of Fitou by the Etang de Leucate, while the largest part is well inland around Tuchan and Mont Tauch. Fitou should be round and generous and often becomes quite gamy with two or three years of bottle age.

The best known producer of Fitou is the dynamic Les Producteurs du Mont Tauch, the co-operative in Tuchan. Their best Fitou is the impressive Terroir du Tuchan.

La Clape

The coast between Agde and Narbonne is very flat except for the fascinating lump of limestone that is La Clape. This is a very dry, rocky area of scrub and vines. There are a number of quality producers here, among them Châteaux Pech-Redon and Pech-Celeyran.

Limoux

Limoux is south of the medieval city of Carcassonne toward the Pyrénées. With its Blanquette, Limoux claims to be the original producer of sparkling wines. In the Middle Ages they used to bottle the wine before fermentation had finished. The cold of winter would have temporarily stopped the process. Once the warmer days of Spring arrived, the fermentation started again, trapping the resulting bubbles in the bottle. Now most Blanquette de Limoux and all of the more recently created Crémant de Limoux are made by the Champagne method.

NARBONNE
James Herrick Domaine de la Motte, chemin de Bougna, 11100 Narbonne. Tel: 04 68 42 38 92. Fax: 04 68 42 38 84. Mon-Fri 0800-1200, 1400-1800. T.F.E. www.jamesherrick.com

LIMOUX
Les Caves du Sieur d'Arques Av du Mauzac, 11300 Limoux. Tel: 04 68 74 63 00. Fax: 04 68 74 63 14. Every day 0900-1200, 1400-1900.

PORTEL-LES-CORBIERES
Château de Lastours 11490 Portel-les-Corbières. Tel: 04 68 48 29 17. Fax: 04 68 48 29 14. Cellar open every day, 1030-1230, 1330-1930. Picnic area. Restaurant 'La Bergerie'. TF.WS.E. www.epicuria.fr/chateau-lastours

TUCHAN
Les Caves du Mont Tauch 11350 Tuchan. Tel: 04 68 45 41 08. Fax: 04 68 45 45 29. 18 Jul-31 Aug Mon-Sat, 0900-1300, 1400-1800, rest of year Mon-Fri 0900-1200, 1400-1800. Fitou, Corbières, Rivesaltes, Muscat de Rivesaltes. TF.WS.E.

VILLEVEYRAC
Abbaye de Valmagne 34560 Villeveyrac. Tel: 04 67 78 06 09. Fax: 04 67 78 02 50. Every day. 15 Jun-30 Sep 1000-1200, 1430-1830, rest of year 1400-1800. 13th-century abbey with cloisters; Gothic church used as cellars. Coteaux de Languedoc. TF.E.G. ☎ E-mail: valmagn@aol.com

The cellars of the Château de Grezan near Faugères some 30km (20 miles) north of Béziers. There is a restaurant attached to the château.

Limoux is also an important producer of Chardonnay, both VDP Haute Vallée de l'Aude and AC Limoux. The cooler climate of this area gives more intensity of flavor to white grapes, so the whites produced here have more flavor and acidity than those of the Languedoc plain.

The Caves de Sieur d'Arques is one of the most dynamic co-operatives and is responsible for a large part of the production of both still and sparkling wine around Limoux.

Roussillon

Although linked administratively with Languedoc, Roussillon has its own distinct identity. This is Catalan France with strong links with neighboring Catalonia. Many road signs are in both Catalan and French.

The table wines of Roussillon are broadly similar to those of Languedoc. The grape varieties used are the same. The emphasis is on reds with some roses and an increasing amount of white wine. But, as in Languedoc, the heat of the summer means that it is difficult to make really interesting white wines. Modern refrigeration means it is possible to make perfectly drinkable whites, but they are rarely exciting.

BANYULS-SUR-MER
S.C.A.E. Parcé et Fils
Domaine du Mas Blanc, 9, ave Général de Gaulle, 66650 Banyuls-sur-Mer. Tel: 04 68 88 32 12. Fax: 04 68 88 72 24. (M. Parcé). By appointment only. T.F.WS.E.S. ☎

CASES-DE-PENE
Château de Jau 66600 Cases-de-Pène. Tel: 04 68 38 90 10. Fax: 04 68 38 91 33. (M. Rouvière). 15 Jun-15 Sep, every day 1000-1900. Art Exhibition, restaurant (by reservation). Côtes du Roussillon, Muscat de Rivesaltes, Banyuls. T.F.WS.E.

COLLIOURE
Domaine La Tour
Vielle 3 Ave du Mirador, 66190 Collioure. Tel: 04 68 82 42 20. Fax: 04 68 82 38 42. 1 Apr-30 Sept 1030-1200, 1430-2000. In winter by appointment only.

MAURY
Mas Amiel 66460 Maury. Tel: 04 68 29 01 02. Fax: 04 68 29 17 82.

Banyuls, one of the great fortified wines of the French Catalan coast, matures in the summer heat.

Valley of the Agly
Supposedly the best red wines come from the area in the north of Roussillon around the river Agly, which is entitled to the appellation Côtes du Roussillon Villages. Château de Jau and Mas Crémat are two of the leading properties here.

Vineyards to the south of Perpignan have to content themselves with being plain Côtes du Roussillon. However, whatever the French wine legislation may believe, the quality of the wine produced south of Perpignan can be just as good as that of its neighbors to the north.

Vin Doux Naturel (VDN)
It is the fortified wines that make the Roussillon really different. They are little appreciated outside France, but the best are some of the most interesting fortified wines in the world.

Misleadingly called *vin doux naturel*, they are not really naturally sweet because pure alcohol is used to stop the fermentation, so the wine is usually left sweet. The strength of the spirit used is much higher than that used for Port, for example. For a VDN the spirit is over 96°, so it is flavorless. With Port, the spirit added is 77° and so it adds a flavor to the wine. Also the proportion added is much lower: a minimum of 5% and a maximum of 10% compared to 20% for Port. This is because the wine is allowed to ferment to around 13°, whereas Port only reaches 8° before the spirit is added.

Muscat de Rivesaltes has become popular outside France over the past 20 years.

The other fortified wines, especially Banyuls, Maury and Rivesaltes, are little known outside France, but they count among the world's most fascinating fortified wines. Domaine Cazes in Rivesaltes, just north of Perpignan, make some of the most complex, especially their Aimé Cazes, which is made from Grenache Blanc. They also make a very good range of table wines both *vin de pays* and AC.

Maury
This small town, in the lee of the vertiginous Château de Queribus, has its own AC for fortified wines. Grenache, which gets very ripe with a high potential alcohol, is the chief variety used. Mas Amiel, the leading property, has one of the most extraordinary sights in the wine world

The Château des Templiers, founded in the 12th century by the Knights Templar, dominates the picturesque port of Collioure.

– a "park" of over 3,000 carboys. Filled with Maury, these are left outside for a year. Exposure to heat and rain gives an oxidized taste, known locally as *rancio*. It takes the whole of June to empty and refill them.

Côte Vermeille

The vineyards of Collioure and Banyuls are some of the most dramatic in France. The very steep terraced vineyards stretch up the coastal hills of the Pyrénées where they meet the deep blue Mediterranean. The picturesque little town of Collioure is famous for its anchovies and artists.

In mid-summer these vineyards are searingly hot as the heat reflects off the schisteous soil. Grenache is the main variety here. AC Collioure is for a powerful still wine, mainly red though a little rosé is made, while AC Banyuls is for fortified.

Apart from a tiny amount of white Banyuls, this wine is either red, if it is made in a young vintage style and bottled early, or a browner hue, varying from tawny to toffee, if it is aged for a long time in large barrels. Although Banyuls is customarily sweet, there are a few examples of Banyuls Grand Cru that are dry.

RIVESALTES
Domaine Cazes 4 rue Francisco-Ferrier, BP 61, 66602 Rivesaltes. Tel: 04 68 64 69 79. Fax: 04 68 64 08 26.
TAUTAVEL
Les Maîtres Vignerons de Tautavel 66720 Tautavel. Tel: 04 68 29 12 03. Fax: 04 68 29 41 81. Mon-Sun 0800-1300, 1400-2000. Côtes du Roussillon-Villages, Muscat de Rivesaltes. TF.WS.
TROUILLAS
La Casenove 66300 Trouillas. Tel: 04 68 21 66 33. Fax: 04 68 21 77 81. Mon-Sat 1000-1200, 1600-1900.

Provence

One of the most regular problems of the wine merchant is that of holiday wines. At the end of every summer, customers come to him saying, "I tasted such and such a wine when I was on holiday. It was sensational. Please will you get some of it for me." Often, these wines are wines from Provence.

There can be few happier memories than that of sitting outside a quayside bar in the South of France, watching the world go by, with a bottle of Côte de Provence rosé in an ice-bucket, and a glass of it in your hand. Sadly, Provence wines are summer wines; sadly, they just do not taste the same in February in Flint, Michigan or Fulham, London.

Nevertheless at the right time and place, on the Riviera in the summer, these wines are enjoyable. Make the most of them while you are there, and visit the vineyards that produce them. Then you will not be disappointed.

Most of the vineyards of Provence lie along the valleys of the rivers Arc and Argens, on the route of the A8 motorway.

Much of the wine is made in co-operative cellars with emotive names like la Prévoyance. Here is made the traditional wine of Provence, a rosé that is high in alcohol and lacking in fruit – whatever defects it may have being masked by the temperature at which it is served.

There is a second band of vineyards along the coast from Marseilles, to Sainte-Maxime and Saint-Tropez. From both these areas comes the ubiquitous Côtes de Provence, too often relying on the novelty of the bottle shape, rather than what is in it, to attract the attention of the consumer.

Nevertheless, there are encouraging signs that growers are beginning to see that the vast captive market of holiday-makers on their doorstep might begin to ask for something rather better. As a result, less emphasis is being placed on the rosé wines (and those that are made are lighter and crisper), and more on

fresh, white wine. The fact that the Côtes de Provence now has *appellation contrôlée* status, with its obligatory tasting, has woken people up.

Red wine, too, is made. The old-fashioned wines are based on the traditional stand-bys of the southern French wine grower, the Carignan and the Grenache, and will probably be bottled in the traditional waisted Provence bottle. Growers who have

To get to Provence
Aix-en-Provence is 754km (471 miles) from Paris and 97km (60 miles) from Orange on the A6, A7, and A8. It is 140km (87 miles) from Montpellier on the A9, A54, N113, A54, A7 and A8.

The picturesque Château Vignelaure in the Coteaux d'Aix-en-Provence.

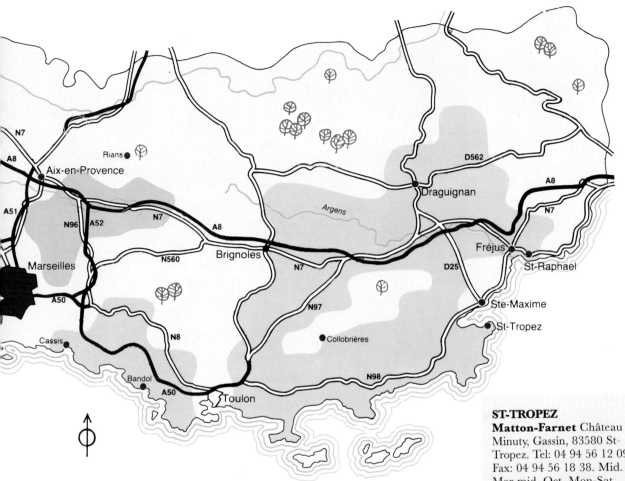

Coteaux d'Aix-en-Provence

Côtes de Provence

planted better varieties like the
Cabernet Sauvignon and the Syrah
tend to use Bordeaux bottles. However,
this simple test is not an infallible guide
to quality! Within the region, there are
more individual wines being made.

Les Baux de Provence

The village from which the name of
this newly-made *appellation* derives
also gave its name to bauxite, the
mineral ore used to produce
aluminum. This is an area where
organic vineyards develop naturally
pure and harmonious wines, without
the use of any inorganic fertilizer.

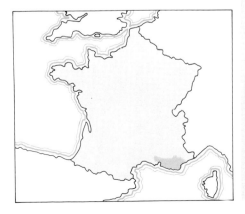

ST-TROPEZ
Matton-Farnet Château
Minuty, Gassin, 83580 St-
Tropez. Tel: 04 94 56 12 09.
Fax: 04 94 56 18 38. Mid.
Mar-mid. Oct, Mon-Sat
(winter Mon-Fri), 0915-
1230, 1400-1900. Napoleon
III chapel. Exhibition of
faïence. TF (TP and
booking for groups) WS.E.
WINE FESTIVALS
Brignoles Provence and Coteaux
Varois Wine Festival, mid-Apr.
St-Raphaël Côtes de Provence
Wine Festival, mid-Jun.
Nice Wine Festival, 1st Sun Aug.
Fréjus Wine Festival, 2nd
weekend Aug.
Ste-Maxime Wine Festival, 4th
weekend Aug.
St-Tropez Harvest Festival
mid-Sep.
Arles *Corrida des Vendanges*, end
Sep.

121

Aix-en-Provence is an agreeable center for visiting the local vineyards. Here, pedestrians stroll beneath the shade of the planes — those most French of urban trees — on the Cours Mirabeau, which leads to the Casino.

Coteaux d'Aix

The reputation of the Coteaux d'Aix-en-Provence, which became an *appellation contrôlée* in 1985, has been growing steadily. Vines have been grown in the area since Roman times. Here a number of growers have built up the names of their properties. This has been done by planting better grape varieties, usually a blend of Cabernet Sauvignon, along with more typical local varieties such as Syrah, Grenache, Mourvèdre. In addition, growers have increased their investment in the vineyards and vinification and have taken greater care over aging the wines.

A limited amount of white is made from Sauvignon and Sémillon blended with local varieties like Grenache Blanc and Vermentino.

One of the best known of these properties is Château Calissanne. This is to the south of Salon de Provence and close to the Etang de Berre. Calissanne is a very large and historic property of 1000 hectares (2420 acres). There are Roman remains, and a Roman road passed through the property. There are 90 hectares (218 acres) of vines planted as well as olives and almonds. The imposing château dates from the 17th century and was considerably extended by an industrialist from Marseilles during the 19th century.

Calissanne is now run by Jean Bonnet who makes nine different wines. His top red, Clos Victoire, is a blend of Syrah and Cabernet Sauvignon, and is aged for at least a year in new oak barrels.

Château de Fonscolombe

Rather longer in wine-making in the region is the family of the Marquis de Saporta, originally from Aragon in Spain. They obtained the property of the Château de Fonscolombe by marriage in 1810. The 170 hectare (over 400 acre) estate lies on chalky-clay soil on the south bank of the river Durance north of Aix. Here, the top wine is sold as Coteaux d'Aix-en-Provence, with as much again as Vin de Pays des Bouches du Rhône and ordinary table wine. Less than a sixth of the red vines planted are Cabernet Sauvignon. The rest are the traditional local varieties – Grenache, Carignan and Cinsault.

As an enclave within the area of the Coteaux d'Aix-en-Provence is the small *appellation* of Palette. The chalky soil gives fuller bodied wines (red, white and rosé are made) than the rest of the region. Production is small, and the one property of note is Château Simone, most of whose wine goes no farther than smart restaurants in Aix-en-Provence and on the Côte d'Azur.

Marseilles

This city was a Greek colony and from the earliest times it was known for its full, rather heavy, wines, which were useful for blending. Where the Phoenician merchants used to moor their galleys is now the center of the Vieux Port. Marseilles has many attractive features, but cannot be described as an attractive city, for the widespread squalor puts off anyone who looks at all closely.

Aix-en-Provence

The same cannot be said about nearby Aix-en-Provence, which was settled by the Romans, largely on account of its warm-water springs.

There are many Roman remains in the region; to the west, at Saint-Chamas, on the northern shore of the Etang de Berre, is the Pont Flavien. To the east of the town, in 125 B.C., the Roman general Marius gained a major victory over the Cimbri, who are said to have lost 100,000 men on the day. It is said that Marius is still one of the most popular names in the area.

Between the vineyards of the valleys of the Arc and the Argens and those of the coast lies the wooded Massif des Maures. From the quiet village of Collobrières at its center, there are many beautiful drives.

A former nunnery, the picturesque property of Château Simone is one of Provence's most historic vineyards, and constitutes two-thirds of the tiny appellation of Palette. Sir Winston Churchill and the painter Paul Cézanne are numbered among celebrated enthusiasts of its wine, which today remains a rarity.

LANÇON-PROVENCE
Château de Calissanne
13680 Lançon de Provence.
Tel: 04 90 42 63 03. Fax:
04 90 42 40 00. Every day
0800-1200, 1400-1800. Olive
oil for sale. T.F.WS.E. ☎

BANDOL
Domaine Tempier
E.A.R.L. Peyraud, 83330
le Plan du Castellet. Tel:
04 94 98 70 21. Fax: 04 94
90 21 65. Mon-Fri 0900-1200,
1400-1800. T.F.WS.E. ☎
www.chateaufonscolombe.com

LE PUY-STE-REPARADE
Château de Fonscolombe
rte de St Canadet, 13610 Le
Puy-Ste-Réparade. Tel: 04
42 61 89 62. Fax: 04 42 61
93 95. Mon-Sat 0800-1200,
1400-1800. T.F.WS.E.

FOR FURTHER INFORMATION
C.I.V.C.P. RN 7, 83460 Les
Arcs sur Argens. Tel: 04 94 99
50 10. Fax: 04 94 99 50 19.

The fishing port (above) and the bay (below) of Cassis, not far from Marseilles.

Cassis, Bandol and Bellet

Apart from the wines that have already been mentioned, there are three long-standing A.C. wines, whose reputation – and price – have always stood out from the general mass of the wines of Provence. All three are coastal wines, and all three are largely consumed in the immediate neighborhood.

The names of the three wines are: Bandol, Cassis and Bellet. Of these, the first is by far the most important, both in terms of production and reputation, but if we continue our geographical progression from west to east, the first one that we come to is Cassis.

Cassis

Almost on the doorstep of Marseilles, Cassis is only 22km (14 miles) away by the D559, which winds across the Col de la Gineste, from where there are beautiful views across to the islands of Calseraigne and Riou.

Cassis itself is a small fishing village tucked away in a small bay. Unfortunately, its proximity to Marseilles means that, particularly at weekends, it is swamped by those coming for the pretty quayside fish restaurants, the casino and the beach. The steep slopes behind, which were once dominated by vines, are being steadily overrun with holiday villas.

FOOD IN PROVENCE

For me, the first thing that the word Provence conjures up is herbs, and they seem to appear everywhere in the cookery, sprinkled on meat before it is grilled, in soups, like *soupe au pistou*, or even in the basic provençal sauce. Tomatoes, garlic too, and, of course, olive oil play major roles in the kitchen.

All of these are ingredients in that Mediterranean specialty, the *bouillabaisse*. To these must be added saffron and a selection of ten or so different fish, plus shellfish. Just as typical is a plate of grilled sardines!

There are certain regional specialties: Aix is known for its sweets, particularly the *calissons*, Cavaillon for its melons and Arles for its sausages.

Perhaps the best cheeses are those made from goat's milk and then matured, with herbs, in olive oil.

Because of its climate, this is a region of simple cookery. The freshest of raw materials are used. In this part of the world you eat outside: what could be better than a *salade niçoise*, grilled fish, fruit and cheese, washed down by a bottle of chilled wine.

Cassis makes red, white and a little rosé wine, the most distinctive of the three being the white, which has a golden straw color and a vaguely nutty flavor.

Bandol

The area covered by the vineyards of Bandol, which is almost to Toulon what Cassis is to Marseilles, is more than six times as large as that of its neighbor. It also has one considerable advantage: for the most part it is well away from the town itself, and the sea, on rocky, limestone soil.

The basic grape variety is the Mourvèdre, for the red wines, and, by law, these must spend a minimum of eighteen months in wood, generally large oak *foudres*. The result is a full, round, opulent wine that has an immediate appeal when young, but which will nevertheless age well.

The red is the best wine, but there is probably more rosé produced, in answer to the regional demand. To my knowledge, this is the only rosé wine that must spend an obligatory period – eight months – in wood, and this tends to give it an orange tinge.

The proportion of white wines made is very small, and I must admit that those that I have tasted have had little appeal.

Bellet

I suppose that the most fashionable, and the most crowded, part of the Riviera is that between Cannes and the Italian border.

With the pressures on land, even up into the hills, being so high, it is not surprising that little wine is made – and most is undistinguished, at that.

Nevertheless, there is one minute *appellation*, so small that it appears on few wine maps. In just two properties in the hills above Nice airport, Bellet is produced in the three colors.

By far the best is the white variety – but then rarity makes for a high price!

Savoie

O f all the vineyard regions of France, that of Savoie is in some ways the most complicated. Indeed, it does not exist as a cohesive group of vines, but rather as a scattering of vineyards in a fish-hook shape, running along the south bank of Lake Geneva, the river Rhône, the Lac du Bourget and the valley of the Isère.

The situation is not made easier, for the wines are named after individual villages, grape varieties, or a combination of the two. While there are some grapes grown, like the Gamay, that are common in the rest of the viticultural world, the majority are purely local varieties or travel under aliases that are difficult to penetrate.

Little of the wine is seen outside the area, for most of it is eagerly consumed in the local ski-resorts of Chamonix, Mégève and Courchevel or in Aix-les-Bains and Chambéry.

DOUVAINE
Stef Mercier Domaine de la Grande Cave de Crépy, Loisin, 74140 Douvaine. Tel: 04 50 94 01 23. Fax: 04 50 94 19 86. (M. Claude Mercier). Mon-Fri 0800-1200, 1330-1900; Sat 0800-1200, 1300-1800; Sun, holidays 1000-1200, 1400-1800. Closed Sep. Historic cellars. TF.WS.E. (☎ for groups).
MONTMELIAN
Château de la Violette Les Marches, 73800 Montmélian. Tel: 04 79 28 13 30. Fax: 04 79 28 06 96. Mon-Sat 0800-1200, 1400-1800. Closed Oct. TF.WS. ☎ E-mail: danielfustinoni@ post.club-internet.fr www.multimania.com/echo73
FOR FURTHER INFORMATION
C.I.V.S. 3, rue du Château, 73000 Chambéry. Tel: 04 79 33 44 16. Fax: 04 79 85 92 47.
WINE FESTIVAL
Chambéry Savoie Fair, Sep.

The Abbey of Hautecombe, by the side of the Lac du Bourget. The vineyards in the foreground produce wines with the appellation of *Marestel.*

Apart from the many variations permitted of Vin de Savoie, there are two villages that have their own *appellation contrôlée*. These are Crépy, on the south shore of Lake Geneva, and Seyssel, on the Rhône to the north of Aix-les-Bains.

Crépy, which comes in a green flute bottle, like that of Alsace, is very low in alcohol and with a refreshing acidity. The grape used is Chasselas, which is generally considered in France to be a table grape. The locals call the wine *Crépy crépitant*; that is, it has a very light sparkle.

The town of Seyssel lies on both banks of the Rhône, with half of it being in the Ain *département* and the rest in Haute-Savoie. Production is divided between still, dry wines and sparkling wine made by the Champagne method. The success of these sparkling wines has overtaken production, and grapes are now brought in from outside the region to make non-A.C. wine.

As for the rest of the wines of Savoie, the rule appears to be that the wine is better if the name of the village appears on the label. Among the better village names are Ayze, Frangy, Chautagne, Marestel, Apremont, Abymes, Chignin, Arbin and Montmélian. These are not to be confused with the grape varieties. Among the lesser-known names here that you might meet are the Altesse (Roussette), Molette, Jacquère and Bergeron in white wines and the

Savoie vineyard area

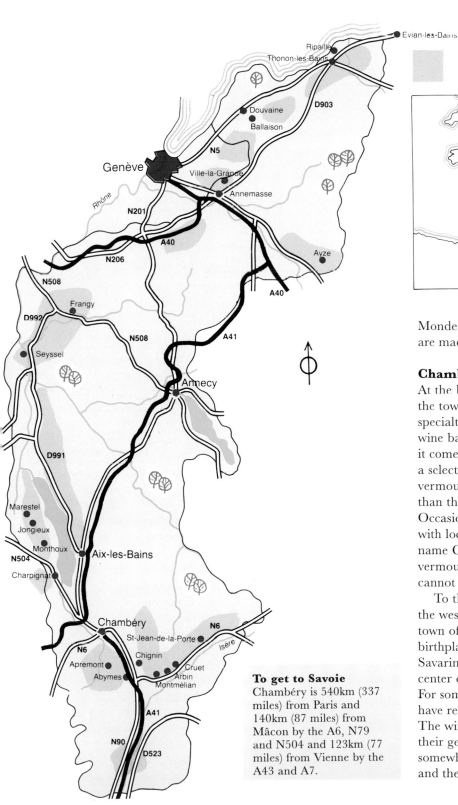

To get to Savoie
Chambéry is 540km (337 miles) from Paris and 140km (87 miles) from Mâcon by the A6, N79 and N504 and 123km (77 miles) from Vienne by the A43 and A7.

Mondeuse in red. Nearly all the wines are made to be drunk young.

Chambéry

At the heart of the Savoie vineyards is the town of Chambéry. Here the specialty is vermouth. Originally the wine base was local, but now most of it comes from Italy. Into this is infused a selection of Alpine herbs, to give a vermouth that is much more delicate than those made elsewhere. Occasionally, it can be found flavored with local strawberries, under the name Chambéryzette. Chambéry vermouth is a protected *appellation* and cannot be made elsewhere.

To the north-west of Chambéry, on the west bank of the Rhône, is the town of Belley. This was the birthplace of the gastronome Brillat-Savarin (1755-1826). It is also the center of the VDQS region of Bugey. For some reason the local growers have resisted taking the A.C. status. The wines, red, white and rosé, reflect their geographical position – somewhere between Savoie, the Jura and the Beaujolais.

Corsica

A hundred and sixty years ago, a French writer said of Corsica, "The vines of this island are remarkable as much for their quality as for the abundance of their fruit. There is very little land where excellent wine can not be obtained, if only it were made with more care."

The same might be said today, though in between then and now the vineyards on the island were totally destroyed by phylloxera. From that time until the French withdrawal from Algeria, viticulture was in decline.

The loss of Algeria had two consequences for Corsican wine production. First of all, there was an immediate need for heavy blending wines to mix with those of the Midi, in order to fill the traditional French liter bottles of *vin ordinaire*. Secondly, there arrived a number of dispossessed growers from North Africa with money in their pockets. Put the two together and what do you have? Large quantities of very ordinary wine.

The chalk hills of Patrimonio, in northern Corsica. This part of the island produces quality white and rosé wines, as well as full-bodied reds.

This situation could not last, however, for when the European Union was created, the way was open for large quantities of high-in-alcohol and low-in-price wine from Puglia, and other parts of Italy, to flow into France. As a result, many of the newly-planted Corsican vineyards were grubbed up and replanted with better varieties. Traditionally, for red wines, these have been the local Sciacarello and the Niellucio. (The latter is a close relative of the Sangiovese of Tuscany.) Also from the mainland have come such southern grape varieties as the Grenache, the Syrah and the Mourvèdre. White wines are made mainly from the Vermentino and the Ugni Blanc.

The dominant geographical feature of the island is the mountains, which come down steeply to the sea, except for one part of the eastern side, where there is a plain up to 16km (10 miles) wide. It was on this plain that many of the larger vineyard properties were created. The best wines, however, come from vineyards planted on the slopes.

Much of the wine is sold as *vin de pays* – vin de pays de l'Ile de Beauté, that is. The best wines, however, are entitled to the *appellation contrôlée* Vin de Corse and there are a number of regional names that can be added to this.

These are as follows, working in a clockwise direction from the northern tip of the island:

Coteaux du Cap Corse (not to be confused with the local aperitif of the same name). Here the most striking wine is a *vin doux naturel* made from Muscat grapes, often laid out on mats to gain extra sweetness.

Patrimonio The oldest A.C. on the island. Here the chalky soil gives deep purple wines with a great deal of complexity, perhaps the best on the island.

Porto-Vecchio from the south-east of the island. Generally the best white wines.

Figari The southern tip of Corsica is very rugged. Excellent red wines with much character are made here.

Sartène Elegant red, white and rosé wines, produced on granitic soil.

Coteaux d'Ajaccio Similar wines to those of the southern Côtes du Rhône.

Calvi Simple wines that should be drunk young. The whites, particularly, tend to lack acidity. Some medium-sweet wines are also made in the region.

Over the past few years, the wines of Corsica have moved dramatically in the right direction. Because of transport problems, few of them will leave the island. They are, however, worth seeking out.

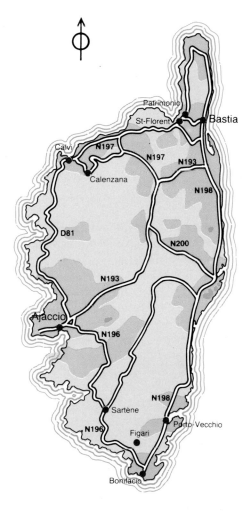

Corsica vineyard area

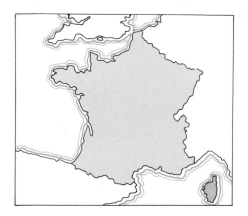

AJACCIO
Comte Guy Tyrel de Poix Domaine Peraldi, chemin du Stiletto, 20167 Mezzavia. Tel: 04 95 22 37 30. Fax: 04 95 20 92 91. Mon-Sat 0800-1200, 1400-1800. All wines have won medals. Large fresco. Vin de Corse Ajaccio. TF.WS.E.

CALENZANA
Tony Orsini Domaine de Rochebelle, 20214 Calenzana. Tel. 04 95 62 81 01. Fax: 04 95 62 79 70. Every day 0800-2000. Vin de Corse Calvi, sparkling wine, aperitifs, liqueurs, jams, nougat. TF.WS.E.

PORTO-VECCHIO
Christian Imbert Domaine de Torraccia, Lecci, 20137 Porto-Vecchio. Tel: 04 95 71 43 50. Fax: 04 95 71 50 03. Mon-Sat 0800-1200, 1400-1800. Beautiful setting. AOC Corse Porto-Vecchio. TF.WS.E.

FOR FURTHER INFORMATION
C.I.V.C. le Santa-Cruz Lupino, 20600 Bastia. Tel: 04 95 30 81 91. Fax: 04 95 30 71 14. www.vinsdecorse.com

Eating in France

One of the greatest pleasures of travelling in France is that of tasting the wide range of foods that are available. The French are interested in what they eat and drink, and this shows at all levels.

One other important point is that children are welcome in all but the smartest restaurants and it is quite acceptable to ask for an extra plate for a meal to be shared – though sometimes there is a charge for this.

Even when travelling on the motorways, it is possible to eat well, and also to drink well – provided you are not driving – for wine and beer can be served if you take a meal. There are a number of chains of roadside restaurants and Courte-Paille and Les 4 Pentes can be recommended for simple grills.

Shopping for food

If you want to picnic, you can probably buy all that you want in a supermarket, but if you want to buy everything at the specialist shops, these are the ones to look out for:
Boulangerie: the baker's. The traditional French loaf is a *baguette*, a *ficelle* is a long thin one and a *miche* is a round one, often made of less refined flour. A roll is a *petit pain*.
Charcuterie: the pork-butcher's. Here you can buy a broad range of pâtés and sausages. Pâtés can be bought by the slice. Often there is also a range of prepared dishes like pizzas and *coq au vin*. These can be useful if you are doing your own cooking. If you want takeaway food, the phrase to look out for is *plats à emporter*.

Fruit, vegetables, cheese, wine and water can be bought at the ubiquitous general stores.

Bars and restaurants

As in other countries, there is a broad range of places at which you can eat. The word for snack is *casse-croute*, and these are available in most bars. Most frequently offered are sandwiches, comprising a large slice of French bread with cheese, pâté or ham. Unless you ask for it there will not be any butter. Also widely available is the *croque-monsieur*, a welsh rarebit, with a slice of ham.

Moving up a stage, there is the *brasserie*, which is generally attached to a bar. Here you can eat a complete meal or just one dish. Normally, there is just one set meal and a large choice *à la carte*. This can be very convenient if there are widely varying appetites in the party, or for feeding children, for food is served all through the day.

An alternative is the *self* or self-service restaurant, now ubiquitous throughout France, and often attached to hypermarkets.

Regional specialties

In certain regions there are regional specialty snacks, which can make for cheap eating. For example, in Brittany go to a *crêperie*, where you can have savory and sweet pancakes, with a broad range of fillings, and a bottle of cider as an economical meal. Similarly, in Alsace, seek out the *tarte flambée*, which is the local equivalent of the pizza.

Restaurants come in a broad variety of styles and prices. First of all, I would suggest that ethnic restaurants, with the possible exception of Italian ones, should be avoided. However much you enjoy Chinese food, for example, I would suggest that you leave it alone in France.

Relais Routiers

For economical eating, but good food, it is useful to look out for the sign of the Relais Routiers. Though aimed specifically at truck-drivers, these restaurants offer very good food at reasonable prices. Whilst the ambience may not be quite what you are looking for, the food will make up for it. Indeed, it is not a bad idea to look out for those places with a lot of lorries outside; the French truck driver places a much higher premium on what he eats than his English equivalent.

The menu

Somewhat confusingly, the French word for menu is *carte*. *Le menu* means a set meal (as opposed to the *à la carte* selection). It is compulsory for restaurants in France to display their menus outside, so it is often possible to do some window shopping, before making a choice.

Again there will normally be a selection of menus at a variety of prices. Often there will be a "tourist" menu (*menu touristique*) at a basic price, which will include a drink, such as wine, beer or mineral water. Sometimes this is hidden away at the back, because, whilst the restaurateur is obliged, by law, to offer it, he is less interested in selling it as he makes a smaller profit. The motto should be, "seek, and you shall find."

There may well be a variety of four or five differently-priced menus on offer, each with a broad variety of dishes. Frequently, nowadays, one comes across a *menu dégustation*, which will include several dishes, but only small quantities of each. This gives you an opportunity of tasting a wide range of the specialties of the restaurant.

At the other extreme is the *menu gastronomique*. This will be more expensive, and as the higher price reflects quantity as well as quality, it should not be attempted by the faint-hearted.

Eating *à la carte*

In addition to the variety of set menus, there will be an *à la carte* selection. This can be useful if you do not want to eat too many courses, but it is generally a more expensive way of eating and, if you do your sums carefully, you may find that you get an extra course free of charge if you take one of the set menus.

By law, restaurant prices now must include any service charge, though it is normal to round up what you pay at the end of the meal.

A few random thoughts ...

In certain of the cheaper restaurants you might be expected to keep your knife and fork between courses, although this practice seems to be on the decline.

You will almost certainly be offered mineral water, *plate* for still or *gazeuse* for fizzy. Only mineral waters in glass (as opposed to plastic) bottles may be served in restaurants.

If you are happy with tap water – and it is safe throughout France – ask for *une carafe d'eau*.

Cheese is served before the dessert, not after it and, finally, whilst the word *crème* does mean cream, it is not often served.

Crème fraiche is sour cream, rather than fresh and *crème anglaise* is custard!

Bon appetit!

French Cheeses

Cheese and wine have long been noted as ideal partners, and it is fitting that France should be almost as well known for the variety of cheeses that it produces as for its variety of wine.

It was General de Gaulle who said, "It is only under the threat of danger that the French will be united. You can't easily bring together a country that has two hundred and sixty-five individual cheeses." I am not sure where he found that figure, but I am certain that it would now be much larger, with the introduction of many commercial brands of cheese in addition to the traditional ones.

The range of styles of cheese available is broad, and while you might expect to find certain cheeses – Camembert, for example – on almost every cheese-board, there are others that have only a regional importance. Interesting, too, is the fact that certain cheeses have their own *appellations contrôlées*, with strict regulations as to where and how they may be produced. Others, and again Camembert is an example, can be produced anywhere, though they will maintain their characteristics wherever their source.

Here is a short list of some of the better-known cheeses of France, and of some of my special favorites. It is always worthwhile asking the waiter, or the shop assistant, about the different cheeses available. In a restaurant, do not hesitate to ask for a selection of cheeses from the board. This will give you an opportunity of making a comparative tasting. One word to look out for, with regard to cheese, is *fermier*. This means that it is farm- (as opposed to factory-) produced and should have more flavor.

(These cheeses are normally made from cow's milk unless otherwise stated.)

Banon (Provence) A small round cheese, wrapped in chestnut leaves, which can be made from the milk of cows, sheep or goats. Mild tasting.

Bleu de Gex (Jura) A round disc with a hard rind. The cheese is solid with a rich blue vein running through it. It can be fairly strong.

Bresse Bleu (Bresse, across the Saône from the Beaujolais) A blue cheese in the shape of a small drum. It comes in a variety of sizes and is similar to a Gorgonzola.

Brie (Ile de France) One of the classic cheeses of France. It comes in the form of a large flat disc. Similar in texture to a Camembert. There are a number of regional varieties. Brie de Meaux is one of the best.

Brillat-Savarin (Normandy) A very rich, mild cheese, high in fat content, with a buttery texture.

Camembert (Normandy) Though coming originally from Normandy, this is now made almost everywhere in France, and, indeed, throughout the world. It is a round cheese with a white downy rind and a fairly mild taste. The name Camembert is not protected, so it can be made anywhere. However, Camembert de Normande is an A.O.C., so cheese with this name must come from Normandy.

Cancoillotte (Franche-Comté) This is a local specialty used for spreading. It has a full flavor.

Cantal (Auvergne) Similar in shape and flavor to a large farmhouse Cheddar.

Carré de l'Est (Lorraine) A smallish, square cheese with a white rind. Rather neutral flavor.

Chabichou (Poitou. Goat's cheese) The shape of a small cone with the point cut off. It has a white downy rind and a pronounced goaty flavor.

Chaource (Champagne) Rather like a much thicker Camembert. It has a pleasant chalky flavor.

Chavignol (Sancerre.Goat's cheese) In the form of a small disc, it has a pleasantly soft, nutty, taste.

Comté (Franche-Comté) A very compact, flavorsome cheese.

Epoisses (Burgundy) A highly-flavored cheese with an orange rind, which is often washed with the local brandy to give it its individuality.

Gaperon (Auvergne) In the shape, and approximate size, of half a tennis-ball, this cheese tastes distinctly of the garlic with which it is flavored.

Livarot (Normandy) Approximately the size and shape of a Camembert. It is distinguished by its brown rind and the "stripes" of sedge-grass with which it is bound. It has a strong smell and a full, spicy taste.

Maroilles (Flanders) A spherical, Dutch-style cheese.

Munster (Alsace) One of the most pungent-smelling cheeses of France. Whilst it has a full flavor, its bite is by no means as bad as its bark. In Alsace it is often served with caraway seeds.

Pont l'Evêque (Normandy) A small square cheese with a golden skin, a rich yellowish texture and full, nutty taste.

Reblochon (Savoie) This is a smallish circular cheese, with a deep yellow rind and a mild, creamy taste.

Roquefort (Plateau of Larzac. Sheep's cheese) The classic blue cheese of France, which is matured for at least three months in the naturally damp caves of Combalou. It has a very full flavor.

Saint-Paulin (Western France) This is a generic cheese made widely in France, based on the monk's cheese of Port-Salut. It has a soft, mild taste.

Bread, cheese, wine and fruit; the ideal end to a meal – or the basic ingredients of a picnic.

133

If not Wine, What?

While this book is primarily about vineyards, and wine drinking, there are regions of France where wine is of secondary importance, and, no matter where you go, there is almost certain to be a local specialty other than the wine.

Beer
As you drive from the Channel ports of north-east France, for example, you are in beer country. The beers of which they are proudest are the *bières de garde*, which are bottled with Champagne corks and are high in alcohol for long keeping.

In a French bar, there are generally two kinds of bottled beer, *une blonde*, which is a lager, and *une brune*, which is a darker, more fully-flavored, beer. There is often draught lager and the normal order is *un demi-pression*, which will give you a 25cl glass. A shandy (beer and lemonade) is *un panachée*.

The other alcoholic specialty of the region is gin distilled from beet. This comes in two forms, young and aged. I must admit to having no experience of it, but I am told that if you want to try the aged variety, a Vieux Loos is as acceptable as anything!

Alsace is the other big region for beer drinking – the skyline of the northern suburbs of Strasbourg is dominated by brewery buildings.

Cider
Normandy and Brittany make up the apple country and cider is widely drunk. Generally speaking, this is drier, and stronger, than the British equivalent (and, for American readers, I should point out that in Europe cider is always what you call "hard" cider). Better qualities are sold in a corked bottle and are known as *cidre bouché*.

Mineral water
One important drink in France, which must not be forgotten, is mineral water. Whilst tap water is always drinkable, and can be ordered in a restaurant by asking for *une carafe d'eau*, bottled water is widely drunk. In the supermarkets, there is a broad range available in both glass and plastic bottles.

In restaurants, the choice is generally restricted to a few well-known, national brands. Local waters are not often offered, except in Alsace, where Carola, from Ribeauvillé, either still or sparkling, is widely available.

Generally, the choice in waters is between still and sparkling. For those who want a clean neutral tasting still water, I would suggest Evian. Alternatives are Contrexéville (commonly called Contrex), Vittel Grande Source and Volvic.

Of the sparkling water, Perrier is perhaps the most common, though, for those who like rather less aggression in their fizz, I would suggest the more gentle Badoit, from Saint Galmier in the Loire Valley.

Brandy
Returning to the world of alcohol, every wine-producing region has its local brandies. In Burgundy, for example, there are the Marc de Bourgogne and the Fine Bourgogne. The first is distilled from the marc, or residue of skins and pips after pressing, and the latter from the lees, or deposit in the wine. Marc is much more highly flavored than Fine and

can be an acquired taste. Other local marcs of note are the Marc de Champagne and Marc de Provence.

Wherever fruit is grown, alcoholic drinks are produced. For the most part these are of two kinds. If the fruit itself is allowed to ferment and is then distilled, the result is an *alcool blanc*, or white spirit. These are produced widely in France, but the finest probably come from the Giessen valley in Alsace. Here, in just a few kilometers, eleven distilleries produce a broad range from raw materials as varied as cherries (*kirsch*), raspberries (*framboise*), plums (*quetsch* and *mirabelle*) and holly berries (*houx*). Other centers of production of fine *alcools blancs* include Fougerolles, in the Vosges, the Rhône valley and St.-Jean-Pied-de-Port in the foothills of the Pyrénées.

Liqueurs

Fruit and herbs can also be macerated in alcohol to produce liqueurs – and these are produced all over France. There are certain regional specialties such as the Crème de Cassis (blackcurrant) and Crème de Prunelle (sloe) of Burgundy and the Génépi (herbs) of the Alps, but there are many companies throughout France, each producing its own range of products. In certain cases, the outstanding brand has managed to create an international reputation for itself. Many of these liqueur distilleries can be visited.

Here are some of the more famous names, available throughout France:

Bénédictine (Produced at Fécamp, in Normandy). A sweet liqueur flavored basically with herbs growing on the local cliffs. A drier version, originally for the American market, is B & B, which has brandy added to it.

Chartreuse (Voiron in the Alps). This is a sophisticated form of *génépi* distilled by the Carthusian monks. It comes in two forms, yellow, which is high strength, and green, which is very high strength. There is also a small amount of old-aged Chartreuse on the market.

Cointreau (Angers). This is the most successful of the *triple-sec* curaçaos. The basic flavor comes from the distilled essence of bitter orange peel.

Grand Marnier (Paris). Another form of curaçao, but using brandy as the base spirit.

Izarra (Bayonne). This is the Basque word for star and has a base of Armagnac, flavored with herbs and honey from the Pyrénées. It comes in both yellow and green varieties.

Marie Brizard (Bordeaux). Whilst this company makes a range of liqueurs and perhaps the top-selling French gin, it is best-known for its *anisette*, or sweet aniseed flavored liqueur.

Verveine du Velay (Le Puy). Made by the Pagès company, which is also known for its herbal teas, this is based on verbena – and an assortment of other herbs.

Vieille Cure (Bordeaux.) Of monastic origins, a herbal liqueur, with Cognac and Armagnac brandies as its base.

A final family in the French world of drinks is that of the *pastis* and *anis* aperitifs, which turn cloudy when water is added to them.

Buying Wine in France

One of the pleasures of visiting vineyards is that of buying wine, whether it be for the picnic lunch that day or to fill up your car for further enjoyment when you return home. Here are a few simple hints.

If you are just buying a single bottle for a picnic, you are unlikely to go too far wrong. However, it is as well to remember that simple food is best accompanied by simple wine. For example, if you are in Burgundy, I would not suggest that you buy anything much more complicated than a Beaujolais, a Mâcon Blanc or perhaps a Bourgogne Aligoté to accompany your *déjeuner sur l'herbe*. The chances of your being able to present, say, a Beaune *premier cru* at its best are small. While it might taste excellent, it deserves better treatment.

Supermarkets

Do not despise the French supermarkets as a source of wine. Over the past few years, they have come to realize that they are capable of selling even the finest wines – and they generally do so more cheaply than even a grower would.

It is always worthwhile looking along the supermarket shelves, for there are often excellent bargains to be found in top quality wines from reputable sources.

How about buying wines to bring home? Not very long ago, there were a number of wines that were described as "not being able to travel." As a class, they no longer exist (if they ever did) but – you should always ask yourself whether it is worth letting the wine travel in the first place!

Before you invest in a wine, try to imagine what it will taste like when you get it home. Far too often, people are disappointed when they later drink what they thought was a sensational wine in a little bar on the water front of a small Mediterranean port, or in some small grower's cellar in the Loire valley.

Wine on holiday

Two things go to make up the pleasure of drinking a wine. One is the intrinsic quality of the wine itself. The other is the atmosphere in which it is drunk. Far too often, where as "vacation" wines are concerned, the second consideration plays too large a part when decisions to purchase are made.

It is no great coincidence that, for example, everyone seems to enjoy Rosé de Provence in the South of France, but that sales of it are minimal in Britain and the United States. The wines are good, but they exist in a "frame" that enhances them, perhaps a little too much. Take them out of that frame and they appear much less attractive.

Another point to consider in a similar light is the quantity of wine that you are going to purchase. I would suggest that when you have decided on the total quantity you wish to take home, you split it between more than one wine. The reason is simple: there is much less chance of the wines being a total disappointment.

Bulk buying

I would also be wary of buying wine in bulk, either in the small plastic barrel, which is becoming more and more widespread in France, or else in a *cubitainer*, which is something like a large "bag-in-box" and which normally holds about 18 liters (about 5 gallons).

In France, these wines are bought for home bottling or large parties, rather than as a regular source of wine on draught. The problem is that they only give limited protection to the wine. As soon as any has been drawn out of the container, there is a real danger that what remains will deteriorate after a short time.

Personally, I always find it safer to buy wine in a proper bottle with a proper cork.

Buying direct

In recent years there has been a dramatic change in the British regulations concerning buying wine from other countries within the European Union.

There are still suggested limits as to what a British visitor to France can bring home. However, in practice, as long as you can show that they are for your own personal consumption, you can now bring back as many bottles of wines or spirits as you like, as long as you have paid the French taxes and duties. The new rules do, however, prevent you from bringing back bottles for friends.

At the time of writing, the general French rate of VAT (Value Added Tax, or sales tax) is, at 20.6%, higher than its British equivalent. However, the rates of duty on wine are considerably lower – about 2.5 pence (about 4 cents) per bottle as opposed to something over a pound ($1.50 plus). This means that there are real bargains to be had – particularly with lower priced wines.

This difference has also led to the creation of a totally new shopping scenario. A number of British wine merchants and supermarket chains have opened branches in the French Channel ports, specifically to cope with the requirements of British tourists. This means that the same benefits can now be gained for Australian wines as for French!

Buying wine *en acquit*

All wine that has had duty paid on it in France will have a government tax stamp on the capsule.

This means that, except in the case of the most expensive wines, which are unfavorably affected by the higher VAT rate, there is now no point in making use of the alternative way of importing wines, unless you are intending to sell them on. If you do want to do this, you must import your wines *en acquit*. In effect this means that you pay no taxes and VAT in France, but you pay them at the full British, or other country's rate. Many producers are unhappy to sell wine this way, as unless you report to the Customs both at the port of departure and of arrival, they are liable for severe financial penalties. However, if you are acting as a wine purchaser for a group of your friends back home, this is the most effective legal way of importing. You also have to state when, and where, you are leaving the country.

Vintages

In most cellars, in most regions of France, you will generally be offered wines of the latest vintage. The further south you go, the less difference there is likely to be between the vintages. However, in areas such as Burgundy, there might be considerable variations in quality from year to year.

Recent improvements in techniques in both the vineyards and the wine-cellars have meant that there is little chance of a truly disastrous vintage, as far as quality is concerned. In the best years, bad wines are made – and vice-versa. I would recommend that you taste before you buy and that you pay more attention to what the grower says than to a vintage chart.

The Top 21 Grape Varieties

Aligoté (white). A secondary grape in Burgundy, where it gives the early-drinking Bourgogne Aligoté.

Cabernet Franc (red). A secondary grape in Bordeaux; more important in the Loire valley, where it produces most of the better red wines like Chinon and Saumur-Champigny.

Cabernet Sauvignon (red). One of the world's great grape varieties. The basis of the great wines of the Médoc, it gives wines full of fruit and tannin, which age well.

Carignan (red). At present, the most widely planted wine grape variety in France, mainly in the Midi. Generally speaking the wine it gives is undistinguished.

Chardonnay (white). Now a world-wide favorite. The quality white grape in Burgundy and Champagne, where it gives full-bodied wines, which are capable of ageing.

Chasselas (white). Largely a table grape. Grown in France for winemaking in Pouilly-sur-Loire and, in decreasing quantities, in Alsace.

Chenin Blanc (white). Also known as the Pineau de la Loire. Used for making all the great sweet wines of the Loire valley, as well as most of the dry ones.

Gamay (red). The grape of the Beaujolais, where it gives a refreshing wine full of fruit.

Gewürztraminer (white). Grown in Alsace, where it gives an individual, spicy wine, often high in alcohol.

Grenache (black or white). Originally a Spanish variety, now widely planted throughout all the vineyard regions of the French Mediterranean.

Merlot (red). The second grape of Bordeaux and the basis of the great wines of Saint-Emilion and Pomerol.

Muscadet (white). Also known as the Melon de Bourgogne. The grape that produces the Muscadet wines of Brittany. Generally speaking, the wines are refreshing, slightly acid, and relatively low in alcohol.

Muscat (white). A highly perfumed grape that is used to make many of the sweet dessert wines of the south of France. In Alsace it gives a full-flavored dry wine.

Pinot Blanc (white). A high-yielding vine making a simple refreshing wine lacking a great deal of character. In Alsace, it is sometimes called the Clevner.

Pinot Gris (white). Grown in a broad range of French vineyards, under a variety of names. In Alsace it is the Tokay; in Champagne, the Fromentot; in Burgundy, the Pinot Beurot and in the Loire valley, the Malvoisie. The wines are generally soft and appealing, low in acidity and often high in alcohol.

Pinot Noir (red). Makes the great red wines of Burgundy and is widely grown in Champagne.

Riesling (white). In France, is grown just in Alsace, where it gives magnificent, full, steely, dry wines.

Sauvignon Blanc (white). Now widely planted in Bordeaux where it is the basis of the best dry white wines. Its finest wines are probably those of Sancerre and Pouilly-Fumé.

Sémillon (white). Used to produce the sweet wines of south-west France, such as Sauternes and Monbazillac.

Sylvaner (white). The most widely planted grape in Alsace. It gives a simple, rather earthy wine.

Syrah (red). The quality grape of the Rhône valley. Now also being planted widely to improve many of the wines of Provence and Languedoc-Roussillon.

Glossary of Wine Terms

Appellation contrôlée (A.C.) The highest regional classification for French wines.

Barrique A barrel, holding 225 liters (222 liters in Bordeaux): the equivalent of 300 bottles.

Brut Very dry, particularly of sparkling wines.

Brut nature Totally dry. No residual sugar.

Cave A cellar.

Caveau A tasting-cellar.

Chai A wine-warehouse above ground, particularly in Bordeaux.

Clairet A deep rosé or light red wine.

Clos A vineyard enclosed by a wall.

Cru A growth, often used in terms of classification; thus, in Burgundy, *un grand cru* or *un premier cru*.

Cuve A vat.

Cuvée A selected vat, e.g. *cuvée exceptionelle*. Can also mean a blend, as in Champagne.

Demi-sec Medium-sweet; generally more sweet than medium.

Feuillette A half-size cask of about 112 liters, particularly in Chablis and Burgundy.

Flûte A tall, slim bottle used in Alsace; a narrow Champagne glass.

Foudre A large oak cask used in Alsace and the South of France for ageing wine.

Frais Cool.

Frappé Chilled (of Champagne).

Glacé Iced (of Champagne).

Millésime Vintage.

Mise en bouteille au Château Bottled at the Château (Bordeaux).

Mise en bouteille au Domaine Bottled at the Domain (Burgundy).

Moelleux Sweet.

Mousseux Sparkling.

Pétillant Lightly sparkling.

Phylloxera An aphid that destroyed most European vineyards during the last century. Almost all vines are now grafted on to American rootstock, which are resistant to this insect.

Pièce A cask, particularly in Burgundy: 225 liters in the Côte d'Or; rather less in the Beaujolais.

Pourriture Noble (*Botrytis cinerea*) A type of fungus that attacks ripe grapes in certain vineyard areas. It increases the sugar content of the grapes, which are used for making the finest sweet wines, e.g. Sauternes.

Rancio A wine that is aged in the sun and becomes oxidized; a specialty of the Catalan vineyards, in both France and Spain.

Sec Dry.

Sélection de grains nobles The highest quality level in Alsace wines theoretically made from hyper-ripe, individually picked grapes.

Sur lie Literally "on the lees." A way of bottling some wines from the Muscadet and elsewhere, where the wines are young and unfiltered so as to give them extra fruit and freshness. Often there is a small amount of residual gas in the wine.

Tonneau A large cask. In Bordeaux, equal to four *pièces*, i.e. 900 liters.

VDQS (*vin délimité de qualité supérieure*) The highest status for French wines after *appellation contrôlée* (A.C.).

Vendange tardive Literally "late harvest:" a term denoting quality, used for Alsace wines.

Vin de paille "Straw wine." A very sweet wine where the grapes, after picking, are left on straw to ripen further. Now made in minute quantities in the Jura.

Vin de pays A classification below VDQS, where the wine comes from a specific region.

Vin de table Table wine. The lowest classification of French wine.

Vin doux naturel (VDN) A sweet dessert wine, often made in the South of France from the Muscat grape.

Further Information

METRIC EQUIVALENTS

Kilometers		Miles
1.61	1	0.62
3.22	2	1.24
4.83	3	1.86
6.44	4	2.49
8.05	5	3.11
9.66	6	3.73
11.27	7	4.35
12.88	8	5.59
14.48	9	5.59
64.37	10	6.21
80.47	50	31.07
96.56	60	37.28
112.65	70	43.50
128.75	80	49.71
144.84	90	55.92
160.93	100	62.14

Hectares		Acres
0.41	1	2.47
0.81	2	4.94
1.21	3	7.41
1.62	4	9.88
2.02	5	12.36
2.43	6	14.83
2.83	7	17.30
3.24	8	19.77
3.64	9	22.24
4.05	10	24.71
8.09	20	49.42
12.14	30	74.13
16.19	40	98.84
20.23	50	123.56
24.28	60	148.26
28.33	70	172.97
32.37	80	197.68
36.42	90	222.40
40.47	100	247.11

Tourist Offices

Look for the sign *Syndicat d'Initiative*. These offices can often help with vineyard visits and hotels. They are pleased to give advice on local events, amenities and excursions and can also answer specific local queries such as bus timetables and local religious services (all denominations). Sometimes, too, they have currency exchange facilities out of banking hours. In popular resorts, *Syndicats d'Initiative* are sometimes open late and on Sunday mornings. Here is a list of some of the main offices:

Aix-en-Provence place Général de Gaulle. Tel: 04 42 16 11 61.

Angers place Kennedy. Tel: 02 41 23 51 11.

Auxerre 2, quai République. Tel: 03 86 52 06 19.

Avignon 41, cours Jean-Jaurès. Tel: 04 90 82 65 11.

Beaune *face* Hôtel-Dieu. Tel: 03 80 26 21 30.

Bordeaux 12, cours XXX juillet. Tel: 05 56 44 28 41. Railway station Tel: 05 56 91 64 70. Airport Tel: 05 56 34 39 39.

Carcassonne bvd Camille-Pelletelan. Tel: 04 68 25 07 04 and (summer only) Porte Narbonnaise, Tel: 04 68 25 68 81.

Chambéry 24, bvd de la Colonne. Tel: 04 79 33 42 47.

Cognac 16, rue du 14 juillet. Tel: 05 45 82 10 71.

Colmar 4, rue Unterlinden. Tel: 03 89 20 68 92.

Dijon place Darcy. Tel: 03 80 44 11 44.

Mâcon 187, rue Carnot. Tel: 03 85 39 71 37.

Montpellier Triangle Comédie. Tel: 04 67 58 67 58.

Reims 2 rue Guillaume-de-Machault. Tel: 03 26 77 45 25.

Saint-Emilion pl des Créneaux. Tel: 05 57 24 72 03.

Strasbourg 10, place de la Cathédrale. Tel: 03 88 52 28 28.

Tours 78 rue Bernard Palissy. Tel: 02 47 70 37 37.

Accueil de France

A further source of information within the country is the *Accueil de France* (French Welcome Office). These offices will also book hotel reservations within their area for the same night or up to seven days in advance *for personal callers only*.

There are not so many of these offices and they are located mainly at important stations and airports. The hours of opening vary considerably depending upon the district and the time of year. Generally the offices are open between 0900-1200 and 1400-1800 from Monday to Saturday.

Shopping hours

Department stores are usually open from Monday to Saturday 0900-1830/1900, closing for lunch only in the provinces.

Food shops normally open at 0700 and may also open on Sunday mornings.

PUBLIC HOLIDAYS IN FRANCE

1 January (New Year's Day)
Easter Monday
1 May (Labor Day)
Ascension Day
Monday after Pentecost
14 July (Bastille Day)
15 August (Assumption)
1 November (All Saints Day)
11 November (Armistice Day)
25 December (Christmas Day)

If a public holiday falls on a Tuesday or a Thursday, there is a growing tendency to *faire le pont* (bridge the gap) and take the intervening day off too.

Sample letter to a grower

[Sender's name, address and telephone number]

[Date]

Madame/Monsieur*, [either or both] Ayant relevé vos coordonnées dans "A Traveller's Wine Guide to France," j'aimerais visiter vos caves et installations le [date] aux environs de [time].

Je serai probablement accompagné de [number] personnes /d'une autre personne *.
[The above paragraph is optional.]

Si cela ne vous convient pas, je vous serais reconnaissant de bien vouloir me le faire savoir, soit par courrier à l'adresse ci-dessus, soit en m'appelant au [telephone number].

Je vous prie d'agréer, madame/ monsieur*, l'expression de mes meilleurs sentiments.

[Signature]

Dear Madame/Sir*,
Having read the particulars of your establishment in "A Traveller's Wine Guide to France," I should like to visit your cellars on [date] at about [time].

I shall probably be accompanied by [number] other people/one other person*

If this arrangement is not convenient to you, I should be most grateful if you could contact me by letter or telephone.
Yours sincerely,

[Signature]

* *Delete where not applicable.*

Using a French telephone

The French telephone numbering system was last changed in 1996. All French telephone numbers now have ten digits.

The system divides France into five broad regions, represented by the first two digits. The code for Paris is 01, for the North-West 02, for the North-East 03, for the South-East and Corsica 04 and for the South-West 05.

The second pair of digits represents the area within the region.

Callers from within France should always use all ten digits, even when phoning from within the same area.

Callers from overseas should dial the same international code as before (00 33), but drop the initial 0 of the area code. Thus, an international call to Champagne, for example, will begin 00 33 3, followed by the remaining eight digits of the number.

In most French telephone boxes, there are detailed instructions in English. Pay phones now work with phone cards, which are available at motorway service stations, post offices and tobacconists.

Further Reading

The sections on France in Hugh Johnson's annually updated *Pocket Wine Book*, as well as in his *World Atlas of Wine*, are invaluable, but the enthusiastic amateur should also be armed with the regional French series published in both the U.K. and the U.S. by Faber & Faber, which includes *Alsace, Bordeaux, Burgundy, The Loire, The Rhône, Sauternes* and *French Country Wines*.

The *Michelin Road Atlas – France* is particularly useful for the motorist, while *Le Guide Gault Millau* will help you locate the best places to eat.

METRIC EQUIVALENTS		
Liters	**US Gallons**	
3.79	1	0.26
7.57	2	0.53
11.36	3	0.79
15.14	4	1.06
18.93	5	1.32
22.71	6	1.59
26.50	7	1.85
30.28	8	2.11
34.07	9	2.38
37.85	10	2.64
75.71	20	5.28
113.56	30	7.92
151.41	40	10.56
189.27	50	13.21
227.12	60	15.85
264.97	70	18.49
302.82	80	21.13
340.68	90	23.78
378.53	100	26.42

Liters	**Imperial Gallons**	
4.55	1	0.22
9.09	2	0.44
13.64	3	0.66
18.18	4	0.88
22.73	5	1.10
27.28	6	1.32
31.82	7	1.54
36.37	8	1.76
40.91	9	1.98
45.46	10	2.20
90.92	20	4.40
136.38	30	6.60
181.84	40	8.80
227.30	50	11.00
272.76	60	13.20
318.22	70	15.40
363.68	80	17.60
409.14	90	19.80
454.60	100	22.00

Index